ELIZABETH HAMPSHIRE

FREEDOM FROM FOOD

The Secret Lives of Dieters and Compulsive Eaters

PRENTICE
HALL
PARKSIDE

A Prentice Hall / Parkside Recovery Book

New York   London   Toronto   Sydney   Tokyo   Singapore

Parkside Medical Services Corporation is a full-service provider of treatment for alcoholism, other drug addiction, eating disorders, and psychiatric illness.

Parkside Medical Services Corporation
205 West Touhy Avenue
Park Ridge, IL 60068
1-800-PARKSIDE

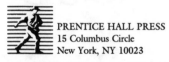
PRENTICE HALL PRESS
15 Columbus Circle
New York, NY 10023

PRENTICE HALL PRESS and colophons are registered trademarks
of Simon & Schuster, Inc.

PRENTICE HALL/PARKSIDE® is a trademark
of Simon & Schuster, Inc.

Library of Congress Cataloging-in-Publication Data

Hampshire, Elizabeth.
    Freedom from food : the secret lives of dieters and compulsive
eaters / Elizabeth Hampshire.
        p. cm.
    ISBN 0-13-334418-5
    1. Eating disorders—Popular works. I. Title.
RC552.E18H35 1990
616.85'26—dc20   89-72212
                                                              CIP

Manufactured in the United States of America
10 9 8 7 6 5 4 3 2 1
First Edition

To John, Daryll, and Kelly

Acknowledgments

I am grateful for the privilege of knowing the seven courageous people who shared with me their stories for this book.

My thanks to Jean Britt for suggesting this book; to Joan Ebbitt for her excellent seminar on the subject; to Bill Mueller, John Keller, Sylvia Shadel, Kathy Leck, and Orv McElfresh for their comments and suggestions; to Kristen Ison, Ellie Cerniglia, Pat Fisher, Georgiana Glennon, Joanne Pompilio and Jill Hart for their heroic dedication to preparing the manuscript; to Nancy Ethiel for sensitive copyediting; to John Small for editing and invaluable support; and to Lloyd Westover for arranging the interviews.

Contents

Introduction

*I*f you bought this book expecting a miracle weight-loss diet, you'll be disappointed. But if you want to stop dieting; if you want to feel good about your natural body weight, whatever it may be; if you want to wake up in the morning and not immediately worry about your weight, your diet, and eating or not eating: then you will learn something from this book. This is the story of seven people who have achieved freedom from food.

The Problem with Diets

Jody dieted for twenty-five years. For most of that time, she "starved" herself just to weigh in at the high end of the normal range on the weight charts. She thought about food all the time, except when she wasn't engaged in some other compulsive activity. She lived at a fast pace, avoided food, and kept her weight down until she found herself stranded at home with her first baby. Then, she couldn't deprive herself of food anymore. Diets just didn't work.

This is a familiar story. Millions of people are trying to solve their "weight problem" with dieting, and it doesn't work. More than 90 percent of the people who diet gain back all the weight they lost, plus a few extra pounds. Obviously, something is going wrong. Is it a matter of willpower? Or is there something fundamentally wrong with the whole weight problem–diet concept? Look at it this way: If any other diagnosis and treatment in medicine failed as consistently and dramatically as this one does, doctors would be sued for prescribing it. Let's face it: Dieting as a "cure" for obesity is an unquestionable failure.

The Weight Is Just a Symptom

But people still diet. It is still prescribed as an answer to a "weight problem." Why? Because nobody questions the assumptions behind it when it fails. Instead, they blame the person: "Poor impulse control," or "lack of willpower" is cited as the cause of failure for most diets. Does that make sense? Can millions of ordinary, earnest people be so lacking in self-control? If so, how do they manage to earn a living or raise children? It just doesn't make sense.

There is another way of looking at the failure of diets as a treatment for a "weight problem." We must simply accept the fact that diets don't work. They don't work because they don't address the real problem. To find a solution, we have to identify the real problem:

> Most people do not have a weight problem,
> they have a behavior problem.
>
> Diets do not change the behavior,
> so diets don't work!

The real problem is not the weight; the weight is just a symptom. It is like a fever. If a microbe attacks your body, in the process of fighting it off your body raises its temperature. You may take an aspirin for the symptom, the fever, but aspirin does nothing to stop the invasion of the microbe. The disease can still kill you, unless you get the antibiotics that do more than just treat the symptoms, that directly attack the disease itself.

Diets are like the aspirin, treating the symptom, the weight, while the illness runs unabated. The real illness is the eating behavior. It is an "eating disorder" or "eating illness," and diets don't do anything about it. That is why diets don't work.

Anyone Can Have an Eating Disorder

It is hard to revise our thinking and look at a "weight problem" as a symptom of a behavior disorder, an eating disorder. It sounds so serious. Denial steps in and says "I can't have anything like that! I just need to lose weight!" But according to the weight problem–diet approach, if you are overweight, it is because you are "weak-willed" or "lack willpower"! Is that accurate? Think of all the times you have faithfully stuck to a diet and lost weight. Hardly what you would called "weak-willed." But then the weight came back. Doesn't it make more sense to look at it as an "eating disorder" rather than a moral failure?

There are many misconceptions about what constitutes an eating disorder. Do you have to weigh 300 pounds to have an eating disorder? No. Do you have to starve yourself to skeletal weight to have an eating disorder? No. Do you have to suffer a terrible trauma or come from a dysfunctional family to develop an eating disorder? No. Many people with otherwise ordinary lives suffer from an eating illness and don't even know what is wrong. They just know that they don't like their bodies and they can't stop thinking about it. They think if they could just lose weight, everything would be all right. They might obsess continually about eating or not eating, going from one diet to another, making and breaking promises to lose or gain weight, and always thinking, "Tomorrow I'll do it."

When most people hear the term "eating disorder," they think "anorexia." Anorexia, however, is only one manifestation of a disease that is far more pervasive in our society than you might expect. An eating disorder (a term used interchangeably with "eating illness") can be compulsive eating, compulsive eating accompanied by self-induced vomiting (purging) or laxative abuse, compulsive eating alternating with compulsive starvation, or compulsive starvation alone. It can be as subtle as the case of a woman of normal weight who is obsessed about her weight, or as severe as that of a man of 350 pounds who continues to overeat even after warnings of life-threatening high blood pressure.

The compulsive eaters have the same disease as the compulsive starvers: they are both addicted. They are both seeking to control something over which they have lost control.

A Disease as Common as the Cold

Many people will read the word "addicted" and say "Not me!" This word has become so loaded with criminal connotations that it is hard to associate it with food. True, nobody ever held up a convenience store clerk at gunpoint for a Twinkie. We have to rid outselves of any such preconceptions we may have about addiction. We must look at it as an illness that is as ordinary and prevalent as the common cold.

We have already determined that many people with a "weight

problem" actually have a behavior problem: Their eating behavior is compulsive. Compulsive behavior is *thoughtless* behavior, behavior that takes place without any conscious intention. Somehow, the behavior, in this case eating, has assumed a life of its own outside the needs and intentions of the person experiencing it. And this behavior involves the ingestion of a substance, food. Whether we like it or not, all of this adds up to a description of addictive behavior. It is an illness or a disease because it is a *destructive process,* with a set of *characteristic symptoms,* the *etiology* or *cause* of which is *beyond the control of the individual.*

Many of the symptoms are immediately recognizable to anyone with a history of dieting. The following list is from Joan Ebbitt's *Eating Illness Workbook* (Parkside Medical Services Corporation, 1987). The symptoms demonstrate how the eating disorder may invade every facet of the sufferer's life: physical, mental, spiritual, social, and economic.

Symptoms of an Eating Problem

_____ Eating for relief.
_____ Starving occasionally.
_____ Always feeling too full after meals.
_____ Feeling guilty about amounts of food eaten.
_____ Clothes becoming too small.
_____ More frequent eating for relief.
_____ Binge eating brought on by certain "trigger foods."
_____ Increasing tolerance for greater quantities of food.
_____ Feeling groggy after eating.
_____ Sneaking food.
_____ Hiding food.
_____ Visiting a diet doctor.
_____ Taking diet pills.
_____ Starving more frequently.
_____ Vomiting.
_____ Others telling you to lose weight.

_____ Avoiding discussion of food problems.
_____ Losing weight.
_____ Weighing yourself daily or more often.
_____ Going on fad diets.
_____ Laxative abuse.
_____ Loss of control over food use.
_____ Inability to stop starving.
_____ Breaking promises and resolutions.
_____ Loss of control over vomiting or use of laxatives.
_____ Rationalizing and making alibis.
_____ Vomiting daily or more often.
_____ Guilt feelings related to eating behavior.
_____ Gaining or regaining weight.
_____ Increased amounts of time spent in bathroom to move bowels.

___ Manual extraction of feces.

___ Feeling ashamed of body size.

___ Changing eating patterns.

___ Exercising to excess.

___ Seeking help from psychiatry, counseling, or group therapy.

___ Work problems.

___ Constant depression.

___ Persistent remorse.

___ Beginning a new diet every morning.

___ Physical problems (stomach, bowel, heart, back, or leg problems, etc.).

___ Constant binge/starve pattern.

___ Moral deterioration (stealing food, etc.).

___ Impaired thinking.

___ Round-the-clock eating.

___ Feeling totally isolated.

___ Obsession with thoughts of food and shame about body size.

___ Eating in the middle of the night.

___ Admission of complete defeat.

First, Identify the Real Problem

You don't have to have all these symptoms to have an eating disorder. In fact, many people only experience a few. But the treatment will be the same whether you are a successful career woman with 20 pounds to lose, a housewife who has a problem with snacking, or a 250-pound bulimic. If you haven't been able to control the eating behavior, it is out of your control, just like a cold or any other disease.

The disease concept is critical to understanding and treating an eating illness. One of the biggest hurdles faced by those who suffer from the illness is the moral stigma inflicted by the belief that they are simply "weak" people with no self-control or willpower. Many people who suffer from an eating illness spend their lives struggling to prove they can do it themselves—lose weight, stick to the diet, stop purging—only to find again and again that they can't. The sense of failure and lose of self-esteem only make it worse. By accepting that they have a disease, sufferers can accept help. By admitting that the eating or not-eating behavior is out of their control, they can "let go" and take the first step toward gaining control—treatment.

Second, Follow a Plan for Recovery

Once we understand the problem, we can treat it successfully. After years of struggling with diets, expensive potions, pills, and various gimmicks, we can stop trying to lose weight and start treating the eating behavior. We can stop talking about diets and start talking about recovery. A diet is temporary and futile. Recovery is continuous and effective. Seven successful recoveries are described in this book. All of them are different but all of them share the same components:

A focus on changing the eating behavior permanently.
A group for support and reinforcement of change.

Various nonprofit, Twelve Step groups such as Overeaters Anonymous (OA), Al-Anon, and Alcoholics Anonymous (AA) played significant roles in the recovery of the seven people whose stories are told in this book. Overeaters Anonymous and other Twelve Step groups are available in most communities and ask only for a small contribution at each meeting to pay for the coffee and the space. They are self-help programs run by and for the members, using principles called the Twelve Steps as a program for personal growth and change. Local newspapers usually list the meetings.

Many mental health clinics and private mental health practitioners also conduct groups for recovery from eating disorders. These usually cost more but are often needed to initiate recovery. The important thing to remember is that you don't do it alone. Not one of the seven people in this book who successfully treated their eating problems did it alone. All the stories describe the same pattern:

- History of dieting, weight loss, or weight gain.
- Lifelong concern and dissatisfaction with body size or type.
- Escalating and futile efforts at weight control.
- A crisis resulting in reformulation of the problem from "I have a weight problem" to "I have an eating problem."
- Group support for stopping the eating behavior and learning new behavior (in all seven stories a Twelve Step group played a significant role).
- In some cases in which the eating behavior was life threatening, inpatient treatment used initially, followed by an outpatient support group.

- Recovery, bringing increased self-esteem, improved relationships, normal body weight, and personal growth.

"Abstinence" is a term that is used frequently in this book. Abstinence means that a person is able to abstain from compulsive behavior, whatever that may be. When Jody, for example, says she finally achieved abstinence, it means she was able to stop her compulsive eating behavior. For Frannie, it means stopping her eating-and-vomiting behavior.

"Recovery" is the continuous process of maintaining abstinence. A diet is just an interlude. Recovery is a state of being. The following list includes some of the characteristics of recovery. Just as the disease involves every facet of the individual's life—physical, mental, spiritual, social, and economic—so does the process of recovery.

Characteristics of Recovery

1. Following a food plan.
2. Gaining freedom from food obsession.
3. Gaining freedom from body obsession.
4. Asking for help.
5. Releasing denial.
6. Emphasizing honesty.
7. Living in the present.
8. Improving physical health.
9. Nurturing the self.
10. Developing appropriate coping skills.
11. Changing old relationships.
12. Forming new relationships.
13. Giving to others.
14. Talking about feelings.
15. Re-evaluating the past.
16. Increasing clarity of thought.
17. Increasing spirituality.
18. Accepting yourself.
19. Accepting natural body weight.
20. Gaining ability to have fun and play.

Find Serenity and Strength

Dieting belongs in the past. Recovery, the growth and empowerment of *you* as a whole person, is for the New Age of today. You will notice that each individual in this book refers to a "spiritual" component in their recovery as part of the Twelve Step programs (OA, AA, NA, and CA) that they rely on for support. As they describe it, the spiritual growth is different from a specific religious experience. It is, rather, a new ability to experience themselves and their lives in ultimate terms. They each describe their spiritual experience as a shift away from a self-centered, controlling vision of life toward a more cosmic view of the self in relation to an ultimate "Higher Power." The new perspective is described variously as "powerlessness," "letting go," "learning to trust," and "self-acceptance," all of which require a reordering of values in which the self is seen less as the center of the universe and more as a part of a larger reality. This transcendence from a controlling way of being (generating distrust, fear, criticism, guilt, and shame) to an accepting way of being (generating trust, faith, love, generosity, and forgiveness) appears again and again in the seven individual stories. It is the source of inner serenity and strength.

Recovery Starts with Treating the Eating Behavior

There are many theories about the causes of eating illness, ranging from lack of nurturing and parental authority, to unresolved Oedipal conflicts, to genetic predisposition, to craving resulting from physiological imbalances. The seven stories of recovery presented here do not address theories of causality. In all cases, treatment was successful without any interpretation of the underlying causes of illness. It is true that Irene feels her family was dysfunctional, Jennifer was sexually abused, Don comes from an uncommunicative family, Frannie felt she was too dependent, and Amy had too much responsibility. All of these problems may or may not have contributed in some way to illness. But the points to be made are that an eating illness can occur without any of these problems, and that recovery starts with treating the eating behavior itself, not with interpreting the reasons behind it. After the eating behavior stops, many problems that were avoided with food are suddenly unavoidable. The Twelve Step programs are designed to deal with most of them. Sometimes, long-standing problems of a more serious nature become available for treatment for the first time. In these cases, individual therapy is needed.

No More Futile Diets

This is a book of hope, a radical new approach to an old problem. After years of hiding under the disguise of a "weight problem," eating disorders finally have been unmasked. No more futile diets. Recovery is possible. The stories in this book describe the problem and the solution. They show that eating disorders can range in severity from Jody's lifelong struggle to maintain a normal weight to Pat's experience with life-threatening multiple addictions. It doesn't matter whether you are an ordinary housewife who can't seem to resist snacks or a hard-driving career person intent on physical perfection. The problem is the same and the solution is the same. And there is a solution!

As Frannie says, "You don't have to live like that. You do have an option." You can accept yourself as you are, you can feel good about your natural body weight, you can go one day at a time without obsession, you can be free!

Preface to Jody

*A*fter years of dieting and deprivation to maintain a "normal" weight, after decades of constant concern about her weight and her appearance, it all felt normal to Jody. Her daily anxiety about weight, her obsession with eating or not eating, were so much a part of her life it never occurred to her there was another way to live. It never occurred to her that dieting was not a solution. She felt all she needed to lose weight was a better diet, more willpower, or to get rid of some problems in her life. She was trapped by her own assumptions.

As her life progressed into marriage and motherhood, it became harder and harder for Jody to diet. At home with small children, she couldn't avoid food. She couldn't control her weight any more. Her anxiety and obsession with her weight escalated. Jody might have stayed in the escalating spiral of body obsession, eating, and dieting with its ever-increasing weight gains if a health crisis had not forced her, reluctantly, to try another approach.

Jody found a new approach that brought her a new life. First, she learned to forget about her weight and focus on stopping her eating behavior. When she stopped her eating behavior with a food plan and help from her OA group, she had to replace it with something. She had used food to respond to life: Bored? A few cookies gave some stimulation. Tired? Try a piece of pie. Angry, hurt, tense? Have some chocolate and forget about it! That was the way she lived.

When Jody stopped using food to avoid life, she had to face it. Her recovery program, the Twelve Steps of Overeaters Anonymous, showed her the skills and gave her the support she needed to deal with life in a new way. As she says herself, "The problems life throws at me still have to be dealt with. That doesn't change. But I've changed."

Jody describes her recovery this way: "I went into the program believing that if I could just be thin, I'd be the person I wanted to be. And I became the happy, self-assured person I always wanted to be and it had nothing to do with my weight! By becoming the person I wanted to be, my weight became what it was supposed to be. And it has stayed there, too, without any starving or dieting or obsessing. I would never have believed I could feel so good about myself without dieting. I feel as though I was a prisoner of food and now I'm free, and I would never, ever go back to the way I was."

Jody's story is a good starting point for understanding why a "weight problem" is usually a behavior problem, and why diets don't work. With Jody we make the transition from thinking "weight problem" to thinking "eating disorder," and from "diet" to "recovery program." The stories that follow Jody will then provide progressively detailed information about the complexities of eating disorders, and describe their successful treatment. As Jody says, "It works!"

JODY

"I Thought I Had a Weight Problem"

For a long time, I thought I had a weight problem. I knew my life would be great if I could just get rid of 50 pounds. I would like myself, feel good around other people, wear nice clothes, do more exercise, go places. Basically I would solve everything if I could just lose the 50 pounds. It took me twenty-five years to figure out that I don't have a weight problem, I have a behavior problem. I eat inappropriately. No diet on earth is going to work because diets don't address the behavior problem. Diets just make it worse. Diets helped me avoid the real problem, temporarily. Maybe I would lose some weight, but I never kept it off. It always came back, usually with a few pounds more.

I probably would have stayed the way I was indefinitely, because it is easier to blame the weight and hope for the right diet than it is to face myself. Diets don't demand any real changes. They are temporary, superficial evasions. Then when they are over, you go back to your old ways. You stay the same, and you end up weighing the same, too. Or more. I probably would have kept on the way I was, except that I accidentally, and without wanting to, found another way to address my "weight problem." And I found that my problem wasn't my weight. It was my eating behavior.

It took twenty-five years to get to that point, and as I said, it was entirely by accident. Because I was so sure that there was nothing wrong with me except 50 extra pounds. I wasn't one of those weak-willed people who went to therapy and wallowed in their problems. I was strong. I was in control. I was coping. I didn't need anyone tampering with my inner me. I just needed to lose 50 pounds and do something about some of the people around me. They were a problem. And that was how I honestly felt, for as long as I can remember.

Starving Down to a Normal Weight

It had always been a struggle to keep my weight down. I went on my first diet at age eleven, at my mother's insistence. I was the only kid in my sixth grade class to chow down at lunchtime with a cup of malted diet drink and a little green salad. All the other kids would be munching chips, peanut butter and jelly, and Twinkies, and never gain an ounce. But not me. I had to starve on 800 calories a day to achieve even an average weight. In six months I was down to an average weight and looked very pretty. I started perming my straight brown hair and my mom bought me some new clothes. I wasn't a drop-dead beauty, but I have big brown eyes and dimples, so I looked pretty good. I remember my teacher saying one day, "Jody, you look very pretty. You've lost a lot of weight." I felt so good. My whole outlook on myself changed. Someone liked me. Someone accepted me. I was okay because I had lost some weight.

To keep it off, I had to starve. As a growing girl, I ate half a piece of toast or a quarter cup of cereal for breakfast, half a sandwich and one apple for lunch, and skipped dinner as often as I could. I had all kinds of tricks. I would buy an ice cream sandwich, peel off the chocolate wafer and just eat the little sliver of ice milk inside. That would be my lunch, but it made me feel good because I was eating something other kids ate. I never drank milk. Too fattening. Now I worry about my bone density and osteoporosis. At a time when I should have been fortifying my bones, I was starving.

It Made Me Angry

But I was never thin. I was like those lab rats that die of obesity while starving to death. I had two tall, thin sisters, so I knew what "thin" was. They ate enormous quantities of food and never gained a pound. My younger sister especially would rush in from school, go straight to the refrigerator, and stuff herself with milk shakes and donuts to gain weight. And she never did. She was as thin as a toothpick. She got to take Twinkies in her lunch and looked like a stick. And I was barely able to keep down to a normal weight on one-tenth the food she ate.

It made me bitter. It made me angry. I felt like a freak, like an ugly duckling. I had to suffer and deprive myself just to be barely accept-able, and my sisters were beautiful and thin and loved without any effort. It got worse later on when my little sister became a cheerleader, a beauty queen and the most popular girl in school without any apparent effort.

"I Never Felt Good Enough"

I had low blood sugar, anemia, was tired all the time, and depressed by age twelve. The doctors saw my low blood sugar in blood tests and would tell me to eat sweet things to raise it. At the time, in the early '60s, that was what they recommended. Then they would tell me I could stand to lose a little weight, that I was a bit chubby. My weight was in the high range of normal, but one me, it always looked chubby. It was partly because of the way weight was distributed on my body. My arms always looked fat. Once I quite eating for a month, only drank a little juice or nibbled a little cantaloupe, and got down to my ideal weight on the charts. And my arms were still fat! So when doctors would say "eat sugar" and "lose weight," when even on a starvation diet I still looked fat, I was devastated. It felt as though I would never, ever, be good enough, no matter what I did.

I managed to keep my weight at the high range of normal all through junior high and high school by simply not eating. I always thought about food, I was aware that I could not eat when everyone else ate. I could not eat the same food the other kids ate. It was a basic tension I experienced every minute of my life. I'd be out with a group of friends, we'd go to a movie and then go to the pizza shop afterwards, and everyone would order some pizza or fries, and I would just sit there, tense. I'd watch everyone else eat while I sipped a diet drink. I couldn't really be a part of the crowd because my whole body and mind was absorbed by my hunger and the tension of resisting it. I just wanted to get away. I started smoking very young so I could have something to do while others ate. I drank enormous quantities of diet cola, which had just come onto the market.

Finding Security in My High School Crowd

In high school I was a crowd person. Even though I couldn't eat like everyone else, I found that if I could be like everyone else, I felt better. I liked the feeling of being accepted. I liked knowing my hair was like their hair, my clothes were like their clothes, my perfume was the same, my slang was the same, we all liked the same people and hated the same people. And here is something we did, that I think all kids do, but which became very important to me. We would pick out certain people, people we decided were weirdos or creeps. Then we would get together and laugh at them and crack jokes about them. It made us all feel cool, I guess, but when this happened I felt especially secure and accepted because I was "in," I wasn't the one that was "out."

After a while, I found I could be very sarcastic, very good at making these sharp, cutting remarks about other people. I didn't think of it as being mean. The gang would all laugh when I came up with these witty little quips. I had a real talent for it. I was cool. I was in control of who laughed at whom. I became a leader. All my bad feelings about myself were gone, directed against other people. I guess I was getting back at everyone who never had to diet, every cheerleader, every beauty queen.

For the last two years of high school I was pretty popular. I was on the yearbook, the newspaper, the debate club. In my senior yearbook, they had a quote under my picture about my "quick smile" and "rapier wit." I had found my niche, although I can't say I had any close friends. I just had a crowd I ran with, and it was very superficial.

Feeling Fat and Inadequate in My Freshman Year

Then when I went away to college, something happened. I had a hard time getting into a crowd. I went to an out-of-state school that was prestigious, but none of my crowd was accepted there. I remember how I felt after my parents left and it was just me and my roommate. The bottom dropped out of my world. My roommate was a thin, cheerleader type who was just happy, happy, happy. She had a closet full of size 6 clothes and a boyfriend who came to the same college with her. She was out every night. She'd come back to the dorm, get undressed and walk around in this gorgeous lingerie without one speck of fat anywhere. I wanted to hide, I felt so fat and inadequate.

I didn't get into the sorority I wanted. I had to go into a lesser sorority that would take me. I felt my whole self-image slip away. I couldn't resist food anymore. I was lost.

For the first time in my life I had an incident with food. I remember it because I never binged on food, so that was unusual for me. I ate half a loaf of French bread with a whole stick of butter and four cups of hot chocolate, and called it a continental breakfast. I was angry. I started to eat burgers, fries, shakes, pizza, all the food other people ate and I never could eat. Beer, pastries, chips, cupcakes— other people ate it, why couldn't I? I was angry, resentful, hurt. If people didn't like me, to hell with them!

I deserved to eat. I had suffered enough, and for what? To be always rejected, never good enough. Years of starving myself had created an overwhelming need, a hunger that was insatiable. I would eat a piece of pie and feel soothed, until it was gone. I couldn't think of anything but food, either eating it or not eating it. It was a constant tension I never escaped. I was never really present in any situation because there was always this tension about food.

I gained 30 pounds in the first six months of college. The only reason it wasn't more was because I would alternately diet, use laxatives, and eat. I rarely ate large quantities. I just ate what other kids ate. When my friends went out for pizza and beer, I too had pizza and beer, for the first time in my life. But the effect on me was dramatically different. My body, after years and years of starving, had lowered its calorie-burning setting so low that I got fat quickly on normal amounts of normal food. It wasn't fair, but that is what dieting does.

Rescued by the Crowd Again

By my junior year, I had adjusted to my new social status, moved into the sorority house, and felt more secure. No, they weren't the most "in" sorority at school, or the smartest or the prettiest. But we did a good enough job of ridiculing everyone else to fortify my low self-esteem. At the time I didn't think I had low self-esteem. What I felt was an inflated sense of superiority which I bolstered at other people's expense. There was the "jock" sorority, all those poor thyroid cases with hairy legs. We had many fun evenings tearing them apart over bridge. But they deserved it, we said. Then there were the "Barbie dolls," the sorority with the thinnest, richest, most popular girls, like my roommate freshman year. We had Barbie jokes: "How many Barbies does it take to change a light bulb? Six: Five to change it and one to hold the mirror so they can see themselves change it." When we would see one of them in some cute little outfit with a gorgeous guy, we would exchange self-righteously disgusted looks.

This ego-bolstering got me through college and made it possible for me to start starving myself again. I got back down to my normal weight but the tension about food was always there, always. I was always faced with eating situations and always tense about it.

The Struggle to Keep a Normal Weight

I majored in business, which was a hard major at my school. I had to study harder than anyone else I knew, and I resented that, too. But I would reward myself after studying with a treat—hot chocolate or a custard pudding, which was a favorite of mine. There was a bakery near campus which made real baked egg custards in little individual pastry shells. I would go over and buy one in advance so I could have it when I finally closed the books at 2 A.M. I wouldn't eat dinner just so I could have that treat.

I met my husband while my weight was normal. He was tall and goodlooking and a regular nice guy. We met at a football game when I dropped my purse from the bleachers and he brought it up to me—just that type of nice, considerate guy. He was an average student, a real joker, and a sports fan. He was fun to be with, always cracking jokes, and had this witty repartee. Everyone in my crowd liked him. They were envious, but not too envious. We got married right after graduation. I'm not going to go into the problems we had planning the wedding, or my in-laws, but it was an incredible pain. We almost cancelled the whole show several times, but we finally walked down the aisle and we were happy.

Frantically Avoiding Food

I can look back and see how Bill, my husband, helped me avoid problems with food. He was tall and thin and I found I could get some satisfaction out of feeding him. When something bothered me, I'd make a gourmet meal and he would eat it for both of us. I call it "vicarious eating." We went out a lot and I gave him my food.

We were very active, out all the time—camping, ball games, swim parties, bridge club, golf, volleyball, everything. It helped me avoid food, even though I hated sports and never bothered to learn golf, tennis, or volleyball. I just went along and watched and entertained everyone with my sarcastic comments from the sidelines. Again, I used my acerbic humor very successfully.

I think the first six years were the best. I loved my job as a marketing manager in a large company. I eventually had a staff of twelve people and I was very busy and I liked the authority I had. Also, my job kep me away from food. I had lunches, but they were usually working lunches and I could distract myself from the food. I still have a few of the skirts I wore then. I know they'll never fit again, but somehow I can't throw them away.

Trapped in My House Alone With Food

Then we had our first child. I had to eat constantly to stave off the nausea, and I gained 50 pounds. After Janice, my daughter, was born, I lost all but 15 pounds of it. I quit my job, I was home all day with Janice, and she was a colicky baby. It was rough. I no longer had all my food-avoiding activities. I was trapped in my house alone with food. I had friends, sure, but it wasn't like they were there all the time. Most of the time it was just me, Janice, and the refrigerator.

Bill was working odd hours and traveling quite a bit. He just wasn't there to help. I was angry about that. He had it great. He was a sales rep and he was out wining and dining clients, staying in hotels, being waited on, relaxing every night with a cable movie, and then breakfast in bed from room service. And I was home with a crying baby who needed my attention at all times. My resistance broke down and I started to eat. Again, not a lot of food, and not any particular food. But I couldn't starve myself. Just eating normal meals gave me another 15 pounds.

I felt awful and I was angry. I knew other women in the neighborhood but I didn't feel I could go to them for support. One woman ran a business at home and had a housekeeper come in every day. She had made it—thin, nice clothes, gorgeous house. Her house was immaculate. I would walk by with Janice in her stroller and see those sparkling windows and just seethe—"Oh, give me a break!"

Then Carol, a girl I had known in high school, moved into a house two doors down. We hadn't been close friends, but at least she was someone I could relate to. She had a son six months older than Janice and she would come over mornings. We sat at the kitchen table and ate donuts and talked while the kids played. She was like me, only worse. She was shy and had no idea how to act in a social situation. She hadn't changed since high school. She even had the same limp, dishwater blond hair she had in high school, and the same weight problem. It turned out that we shared quite a few opinions—she resented her husband, the neighbors, and her in-laws as much as I did. She was a very angry person, only much nicer about it than I was. I decided I was in better shape than she was. "Boy, does she have a self-esteem problem," I thought. But we got together regularly and criticized everyone and everything. I started to diet again.

Food Was My Escape

Then our second child came along, two years after Janice. We planned it. We wanted a boy and we got one. Robbie is a great kid. But again I gained a lot of weight, and 20 pounds of it stuck. I was now 50 pounds over the average weight for my height. I hadn't been what you'd call thin to start with, so I looked horrible. I hated myself. I threw out the scales and I wouldn't have a full-length mirror in the house. I wouldn't buy clothes—couldn't stand to see myself in the mirror. So I just wore maternity clothes and hid my body. I looked worse than Carol. And with a toddler and an infant, I had no escape. Food was my escape. It was the only thing I had to make myself feel better.

People without kids don't know and people with older kids forget the drudgery, the exhaustion, the stress, the desperation of being housebound with two small, helpless people who aren't even rational yet. The demands that are made on you exceed anything else in your experience. You have to deny your own needs, even the most basic ones, when they come into conflict with your child's needs. You have to defer your own needs and take care of your child because the child is helpless and you are responsible. You have to do this even when you are exhausted, even when you are sick, even when you are stretched to your psychological limits. You have to put your own needs and feelings aside and be there for your child—patient, giving, and loving.

A Steady Stream of Stress Reducers

It didn't take long for me to start to eat after Robbie was born. The kids took everything I had. There was nothing left for me. I got no breaks. I had to have something for myself, some relief. Something to reduce the stress, to help me stop feeling so deprived. And with kids, food is around all the time. If I could manage to stay awake after the kids went to sleep, I'd sit down and finish off dessert. Just a moment of satisfaction when I hadn't had one moment for myself all day. I never even got to go to the bathroom in peace—either one of the kids would come in with me and start wrecking the cupboards or emptying the drawers, or one of them would be standing outside the door, screaming and trying to kick down the door to get in. And when both kids are screaming and the phone is ringing and the washer buzzer goes off because the laundry is off balance, you have to do something to alleviate the stress. A handful of M&Ms would do it, if only for a moment. At least it was one good moment. And I gave myself as many of those as I could because I needed them and I deserved them.

Many nights I would be exhausted, sitting at the kitchen table and just crying in despair. I could not escape. I hated myself. I didn't want to be fat, but I was trapped. I wasn't a binge eater. I didn't go for the "big fix." I was more like someone on an I.V., a steady stream of little stress reducers—a few M&Ms here, some cookies there, a bite of a donut, even a taste of the kids' cereal as I cleared off the table.

"I Thought I Was Coping"

I think everything really went downhill after Robbie was born, although I couldn't see it at the time. I was just buried in it. I thought I was coping. Carol came over regularly, but I started withdrawing from her because I didn't want to feel obligated to her. But we did things together—went to the grocery store or took the kids out to a fast-food place for lunch. Sometimes I thought she was pathetic—she had so many problems.

Some of the other women in the neighborhood would call from time to time, but frankly I couldn't stand them. They were all so full of it. One of them got a fur coat for Christmas and I thought, "Here I am scrimping and saving for a new vacuum cleaner and she's prancing around in mink!" I just couldn't take it. She invited us over for dinner once but I told her we already had plans. I just couldn't stand to listen to them talk about how good they had it. They were "dinks"—double income, no kids. She called a few other times with invitations, but I always managed to forget about them.

When the kids got a little older, Janice in first grade and Robbie in preschool, I got active in a civic organization and that helped. It was like a sorority only with a charitable purpose. I had a position on the board and had quite a bit of control over the activities. I was good at that. The organization raised a lot of money during that time. In fact, during this time I felt I was finally back in control. Bill usually did what I wanted him to do when he was home, mostly out of guilt. He owed me that, I told him. The kids were very much under control. I was very strict and quick to punish. I didn't allow any arguing or discussion. I thought, "If you let them do it when they're little, when they are sixteen they'll be doing whatever they want." So I ran a tight ship.

"What Could I Do Except Eat?"

But I wasn't in control of food. I started eating larger quantities. It sneaked up on me. I thought it was because of the kids. They were always eating—meals and then morning and afternoon snacks. You have all this food around for them, and they don't finish it, and you find yourself eating it rather than throwing it away. And Bill always wanted dessert—he could eat it. So I made it for him. And there would always be a little left over. Not enough for everyone for the next day, not enough to justify keeping it, but too much to throw it away. So at night, when I finally had some time to myself, I'd finish it. I'd start with one piece of cake, one slice of pie, one brownie. But one was never enough. I'd just finish up what we had.

Food was my tranquilizer. I was grazing all day and eating at night. I had to do something. There were a million problems in my mind: my weight; my neighbor with the fur coat; the pediatrician's ridiculous fee for an office visit; the women at the spa in those little spandex outfits; Bill staying in nice hotels, getting waited on; my in-laws; the utility company rates; the government running the nation like a country club; the asteroid belt throwing a killer meteor at the earth without warning; the sun, which was going to blow up some day. What could I do about all this except eat?!

One summer I joined a spa. Yeah. Joined the only one in town without a baby-sitter. Went three weeks and quit because it was too hard to find a sitter. I laughed at all the women there. What were they trying to prove, jumping around to frenetic music like wrinkled cheerleaders? Grow up!

A Medical Intervention

I probably would have gone on like this indefinitely, but something happened. I went to my doctor for a routine checkup and he said my blood pressure was dangerously high. It had always been on the high side—it runs in the family—but it had shot up to something catastrophic. I was only thirty-five years old. He started me on medication and said I had to lose 60 pounds immediately. He put me on a closely supervised fasting diet of liquid protein. He said I had to do this or risk a fatal or debilitating stroke. If that wasn't enough, he required me to go into a program to change my eating behavior.

Looking back, I am grateful to this doctor. He was young and very progressive. He gave me a choice of two programs. He said the diet was only a "crisis intervention" and that I needed a program for the long term. So I picked the one that I thought would be the easiest, that didn't require me to weigh in or eat special foods or anything like that. It gave me control over the food I picked and I was already looking ahead to when I would be eating again. It was called Overeaters Anonymous. I liked it because it let me pick a food plan and "commit" my food one day at a time. I thought I would go and just ignore all the mumbo-jumbo about the Twelve Steps, humility, and "Higher Power."

I Thought I Was in Control

I went and I hated it. At first glance, it looked like an average group of women. Some were thin, some were heavier than I. Then they started to talk and I was totally turned off. All those poor, pathetic creatures talking about their "character defects" and "powerlessness." I knew I was not powerless. I was in control. And if I had defects, I certainly wouldn't wallow in them in front of other people. They talked about themselves so freely that it embarrassed me, as if they thought everyone there would forgive them and tolerate them. How dare they expect me to tolerate their weaknesses? I remember one very attractive woman there in a designer suit who cried. That irritated me to no end, that display of emotion.

Of course, I thought, I wasn't like them. I would listen and distance myself from them. Powerlessness? I wasn't powerless. I was strong and in control. Ask for help? I needed to lose 50 pounds, not give myself up to some voodoo they called "Higher Power." They kept talking about "character defects." Well, I knew my only defect was that I weighed 50 pounds more than I should, and I was perfectly able to change that by myself. And as soon as I had lost it, I was going to say goodbye to this silly group. They said they had an "eating disorder" and I knew I had no such thing. I didn't have a disease, I had the willpower to lose weight, and I was doing it! They talked about "abstinence." That really got me. Well, I knew about abstinence. I went without solid food for two months, and *they* were going to tell *me* about abstinence!? It was too much.

But I did feel better sitting there and hearing the other women. "At least I'm not as sick as they are," I thought. "This is for really messed-up people."

My Illusion of Control Is Threatened

Then, towards the end of the fast, when I was just starting to introduce small amounts of solid food again, two things happened: My son got into some minor trouble at school, and I found out my husband had an affair. Now, this could happen to anybody. These two things are not uncommon. But not to me. I had an illusion of total control over my life and this cracked it a little. I was able to deny most of the implications in my son's behavior. The school psychologist talked about being "less controlling" and "more connected" with him, which made no sense at all to me. I walked away, dismissing it as psychological nonsense, and decided Robbie needed more, not less, discipline.

But with Bill's affair, it was harder to deny. I knew he was at fault. I knew I was the innocent victim, and he was the bad guy. But the thing I could not get over was that he had had the affair for *three years* and I never even had one suspicion of it. It never occurred to me that he could be so totally out of my control.

I Needed to Eat

I found out about it when it was over. I found a letter from his lover when I went through his briefcase, looking for a pad of paper. I remember sitting on the bed, reading it, and hearing the kids playing outside, and feeling that everything I knew was unreal. Then the next thing I remember is standing at the kitchen counter eating ice cream out of the carton with a fork. I got terribly sick because my stomach couldn't take it after two months of fasting, and I threw up in the kitchen sink. Then I sat down and ate the rest.

I had Bill move out for a week. But there was never any question about a divorce. I was terrified of a divorce. I couldn't imagine living alone, a single parent, living on a shoestring, and working full time and raising kids. I was very angry but afraid to lose him. I kept wondering if she was thin, and it actually made me feel better to find out that she wasn't. But I was in shock because I think for the first time I realized he was a separate person I had not been able to control.

I needed to eat. I was at the part of the fast where they were introducing solid foods and I began to introduce foods my doctor never contemplated: a few M&Ms, half a cookie here or there, the kids' gummy bears. And I made a custard pie which I ate myself—not all at once, but in small amounts over a few days. I was about to ruin two months of a carefully monitored fast, and I couldn't help it.

The Illusion Shatters

I went to an OA meeting the week Bill was banished from the house. I talked about myself for the first time, really talked honestly. But I didn't talk about my eating behavior and my inappropriate use of food. I raged about my husband, complained about my son, found myself pouring out all my anger and resentment about everyone and everything. Everyone just listened. Then the person who followed me talked about the time she had to face her powerlessness. That just made me livid. "These apathetic women," I thought, "unable to take control of their lives, just being pitiful." I couldn't take any more. I interrupted with an angry tirade about taking over one's life and doing something about it instead of giving up. Then the chairman, who later became my sponsor, said very quietly, "Are you in control of your life, Jody?" And I shouted, "Yes!" And then I thought of my husband and son and the neighbors and I started to cry. Something just broke and I started to cry. I left immediately, I was so humiliated.

I cried all the way home. I stopped at a convenience store and got one of those packaged apple pie pastries and ate it in the car. I got myself under control and managed to keep it when the kids came home from school but after I put them to bed that night I sat in the kitchen and cried some more. I needed to eat and I started on the leftovers in the refrigerator. Then Pat, the OA chairman, must have known by some psychic ability what was happening, because she called me to talk about the meeting. Her timing was perfect; she got to me when there was a crack in my facade, and I was actually able to hear her.

Finally Facing the Facts

We talked for about three hours. I can't repeat word for word what she said, but I remember the substance of it.

We talked about control, and how controlling isn't living. Life isn't manipulating, pulling the strings of everything and everyone around you. It isn't making people do what you want. It isn't a situation to be manipulated and mastered. Ultimately, the only thing we have the ability to control in our lives is the choices we make for ourselves. I am responsible for my own choices. Other adults are not responsible for my choices, and I am not responsible for theirs.

Powerlessness was another part of this. I had to look at the last 25 years and see that I was powerless over food. By trying too much to be in control, I was out of control. I was trying to control everyone and everything, and of course I couldn't. And when I couldn't, I ate. I used food as a tranquilizer. Not only that, food was a control issue, too. I was obsessing about it day and night, either obsessing about eating it or obsessing about not eating it. My looks, my body also became a control issue. I was using my weight as a scapegoat for everything I couldn't control, feeling "I could make everything be all right if I were thin!"

I was a person who was out of control and trying to control everything. It really was a sort of insanity, but it was hard to see for a long time because, let's face it, our society worships control! To a lot of people, what I was doing was normal! I got rewarded all my life for my sarcastic, angry comments about everything from the utility company down to the neighbor's clean windows. It was the first time I realized that I had a problem, and it wasn't my neighbors and it wasn't my weight. It was my behavior.

Stop the Controlling, Start Accepting

We talked about accepting myself as I was. Pat said that until I did, I could not accept other people. I realized that every one of the women in the group whom I had criticized for having problems had talked about a problem I had myself. I hated myself for my problems, so I denied them in myself and hated them in other people. Until I could accept myself, I would never be able to accept anyone else.

I thought how my friends were always people I pitied, people I didn't respect, people I thought were worse than me, like Carol. I thought about how angry and resentful I was toward people who were happy, people I thought were "lucky" or had "no problems." I realized there wasn't one person in the world I really liked, not even me. Pat said that would change, when I accepted myself.

Pat kept bringing up denial, and how that kept me distant from myself and from others. She said I wouldn't need it if I could accept my powerlessness over food and face myself. I said I would try. She told me that was all I could do, that there was no magic, and that it was a long process. I had used food inappropriately all my life because I didn't know what else to do. But now I was going to stop doing that, one day at a time. I would change my eating behavior one day at a time by choosing my food each day and asking for help.

Stop Using Food to Avoid

This was when I realized that abstinence wasn't starving or fasting. It was living without abusing food. It was responding to life directly, instead of avoiding it with a few well-timed M&Ms.

I had never, ever suspected or thought that my eating behavior was the problem, and that I needed to address it. I always thought it was my weight. "If I got my weight under control, everything would be fine" is what I thought. I thought that if I were thin, I'd be happy, I'd be the person I always wanted to be, I wouldn't want to eat, I'd be living a new life! Well, I had it backwards. Those things don't come with being thin. First I had to make myself happy by accepting myself, as I am, complete with the body my genes gave me. I had to accept the whole me, learn to love myself as I was, stop denying all the parts I didn't like and do something about them, and stop using food to avoid myself. I had to stop starving, too. Depriving myself of food only made me more angry and resentful. By eating with sanity and treating my body with respect, my body would assume a healthy size and form over time. It would be the size and form it was meant to have, not the one fashion says it should have or that I always wanted, but it would be mine. Uniquely mine. And that was what the program was all about.

I had been using food to deal with life. When I stopped the eating behavior, I would have to find another way to respond to life. If I didn't, I would just go back to the old behavior. Pat said that OA would support me, the Twelve Steps would show me new ways to be. She said, "Just go one day at a time, don't try to do everything at once."

I didn't understand everything she said that night, but I got some little insights that I could hang onto. I didn't realize it, but it was the first step towards being the person I always wanted to be.

I Learned to Ask for Help

As I attended the meetings and worked through the Steps, I began to feel some changes. The first meeting after that was hard, probably the hardest thing I ever had to do was to walk back into that group of people. But Pat was with me and she reassured me that nobody would laugh or jeer or say "I told you so." In fact, everyone was genuinely glad to see me and seemed very happy that I was finally willing to work through the program. It took me a while, but I got over my guilt about my behavior. That was a big lesson—forgiving myself.

Change is difficult. It is very difficult. But it is easier if you have support, and OA gave me the support. I was lucky to have Pat because she was very firm in her Twelve Step recovery. She also has a great sense of humor and, believe me, that is essential.

The first part, selecting a food plan, committing my food one day at a time, was easier for me because I was coming off a fast and learning to eat all over again. And I had sound medical advice that this was a life-or-death situation for me. I gave up trying to do it all by myself. I called Pat or someone else in the group when I wanted to eat inappropriately. I called every day for eight months. After a while, just knowing I could call stopped me from eating inappropriately.

It was hard to find a new way of responding to life situations without eating. I had to change my assumptions about myself and the world, and I'm still working on it.

Working Out My Own Program

First, I had to figure out that it is my job to take care of me. That is exclusively my job. I can ask for help, but that is my job. I can't expect people to read my mind. And if someone can't do what I want, that is no personal comment on me. I had to stop taking everything personally and establish some boundaries. I was using food to put up a sort of sensory barrier or boundary. When I stopped that, I had to learn another way. And the other way is what I learned in the Twelve Steps—to focus on me, work out my own program. If my neighbor is thin, that doesn't mean she thinks I'm fat. If my friend is successful, that doesn't make me a failure. If someone else's house is clean, that doesn't mean they want to make me feel like a slob. This was a whole new world to me. I stick to my food plan, I work through the Steps, I go to meetings, I address my own life. I don't waste my energy trying to work through someone else's program, or expect anyone else to work mine for me. I don't measure myself against other people. I just accept myself as I am.

When I think of all the nice, interesting people I've hated or rejected because they were threatening to me, I feel sorry. But I've learned something, and gradually, as I accept myself and like myself, I can have friends I don't pity or dislike or control.

Now that I don't numb my feelings with food, I have to examine them and respond to them. Is it something within my power? If so, I take some action. If not, I try to let it go. That is the hardest part. Letting go is a mysterious art to me, but it has happened occasionally, so I think I can learn it. I used to just eat away an anger. Now I try to either do something constructive about it or let it go.

I like my new way of living. I've found I can be closer to people when I am taking care of myself. I don't get so angry at my children or my husband. I'm getting to know them in a new way. I found that I hadn't seen them or heard them for a long time, I was so busy trying to make them over into extensions of me. It has been hard, but I'm learning to let them be themselves, and I'm finding that I like them. And I don't try so hard to control every little thing. I was wasting a lot of energy trying to control things I didn't have to control.

A New Life

Gradually I'm becoming aware of all the many and varied inappropriate roles food plays in my life, having nothing to do with sustaining it. Obviously, it was a tranquilizer. But it was also a power object, something I manipulated to feel in control by either eating it or not eating it. It was also a reward, a celebration, or something that marked an occasion. I've had to be more active, explore other ways of doing things. I celebrate now with having friends over, making a card, a picture, or something creative. I reward myself with a good book, a facial, or an hour with a workout coach. Yes, I've started exercising and using my body, and I love it. It's a part of me I'm learning to enjoy.

I also ate out of boredom. That is easy to do when you are stuck at home with kids. I've learned to organize my time for other activities. I'll go to a movie, plant a flower or shrub, do some project around the house, call a friend long distance, arrange some cut flowers, go to the park with the kids, do a craft project with them, ride bikes, read stories, play a game, do a family project. You see, once I stopped eating for recreation, I was freed up to do a lot of things that I like and enjoy. I was surprised at how passive I had been after years of food obsession. Housework used to be overwhelming—how could I ever get it done? Everything would pile up while I worried about it and nibbled. Now, I just do it and it is surprisingly simple.

At first, I didn't think I could stay on a food plan or remain abstinent unless my children and husband did, too. I thought it was impossible unless there were some tricks to it that nobody was telling me about. Well, it is possible and there are no tricks. I'm not saying it is easy, but it gets easier and, after a few years, it comes naturally to me. There are still cookies, occasional cakes or pies, and others among my old "trigger foods" around the house for my children and husband. That hasn't changed. But I have changed. I have accepted that I don't eat those things. I can't eat them without abusing them so I don't. I don't feel deprived anymore. It's like accepting that you are diabetic or have allergies. It is just part of my life now.

Self-Respect, Dignity, and Inner Strength

I have a self-respect and dignity that I never had before. I thought I would get it by losing weight and being thin, but I got it by accepting myself and developing myself as is. I have an inner peace, a feeling that I belong, I have a place in the world. And it comes from inside me, it isn't something other people have to give me. I am still 15 pounds heavier than my "ideal weight," but that's okay. I'm fine as I am. I weigh what I'm supposed to weigh. I'm starting to realize what my "Higher Power" is. At first, it was the program. I let the program help me and support me. I let my sponsor help and support me. I was letting something outside myself help me to find my own inner strength. Gradually I began to feel that there is a whole universe out there, something bigger and greater than I, and I'm willing to be a part of it. Call it life, call it the cosmos, the great spirit, God, whatever. As I have stopped trying to control everything, I've learned to share and participate and be a joyful part of life, and stop being afraid of it. I belong here. This feeling of accepting and being accepted on some metaphysical level is what I call the "spiritual experience" of the Twelve Steps. I am not a religious person, but you don't have to be religious to get this. You just have to be willing to expand your mind and your heart.

I Became the Person I Wanted to Be

You know, this is so ironic. I went into the program believing that if I could just be thin, I'd be the person I wanted to be. And I became the happy, self-assured person I always wanted to be, and it had nothing to do with my weight! By becoming the person I wanted to be, my weight because what it was supposed to be. And it has stayed there, too, without any starving or dieting or obsessing. I would never have believed I could feel so good about myself without dieting. I feel as though I was a prisoner of food, and now I'm free, and I would never, ever go back to the way I was. I'm grateful for the program and grateful for my recovery. The problems life throws at me still have to be dealt with. That doesn't change. But I've changed.

I imagine that many people, hearing my story, will say, "My problems aren't that bad, I don't want a new life, all I want is a diet that works!" Well, at best, only about 10 percent of the people who diet are able to take it off and keep it off. Because the unpleasant truth is that most weight problems are not problems a diet will solve. They are actually behavior problems that can be addressed only by a program of personal growth and change. They are problems of body image and unrealistic expectations and conflict resolution and low self-esteem. None of those issues are addressed by a diet. You go on the diet, you lose the weight, you keep your old ways of thinking and responding, and you go back to your old weight. Meanwhile, people are making millions on diet products. Maybe someday our society will stop falling for the diet trap. For me, I'm working the program, enjoying my healthy body, and grateful for the changes in me, one day at a time. It works!

Preface to Irene

*I*rene's story contains all the basic elements of an eating disorder. Her earliest memories are of "Great Moments in Eating." As she grew older, her mother put her on diets, and eating became a source of conflict. One of the components of an eating disorder is a distorted body image: seeing oneself as being either larger or smaller than one's actual size. Irene's response to increasing stress from her weight gain was denial—she did not actually perceive herself to be as large as she was. But, as she says, "There was always the thing about the weight; it was always the thing."

As Irene matured, she increasingly turned to food to relieve her feelings of inadequacy or stress. With every significant life event—college, leaving school, looking for work, marriage—her eating compulsion intensified. She experienced extreme fluctuations in weight as she alternately starved herself on dangerous diets or binged on sugar-rich foods.

As her weight escalated, she became physically impaired, but her ability to deny or rationalize her true physical condition became more powerful. "I kept this grand illusion," she says, "that if I didn't wear pants, it wouldn't show." At a weight of 225 pounds, that is quite a remarkable illusion.

Irene's relationships with other people, including her husband, became less and less significant as her eating occupied more and more of her life. Every desperate attempt not to eat ended in failure. Finally, she was totally consumed by her obsession with eating or not eating. Her life was out of control, and suicide was constantly on her mind.

Irene tried Overeaters Anonymous at this point because she had heard that it was for people who were "really sick." She had to hit bottom and recognize, however vaguely, that she was not able to control her eating before she could take the steps toward recovery. Her first tentative contact with OA is typical, and her struggle toward abstinence is an accurate account of the process of recovery. It is a process of learning to accept oneself, of learning to be honest, and paradoxically, of "letting go."

Just as all the characteristics of an eating disorder are present in Irene's story, so are the characteristics of recovery. As she puts it, "Freedom from the bondage of compulsive overeating" enabled her finally to life a full life, one in which food plays a role in proper proportion to everything else life has to offer. Once food was put in its proper place, other elements in her life, particularly her relationships with other people, were thrown into stark relief and had to be dealt with. Previously, eating or not eating had provided a sort of sensory barrier against the painful or unpleasant feelings generated by unsatisfactory life experiences. With that barrier removed, she was confronted with many painful realities that she chose to deal with in individual therapy. Therapy does not replace her OA program but is another part of her recovery process.

It is not unusual for a person recovering from an eating disorder to go through profound changes in his or her relationships with friends and family. Irene talks at length about her reevaluation of her family and her new awareness of their roles in her life. It is clear that she would rather "see things as they really are," however painful that may be, than to return to the systems of denial and dishonesty that were part of her substance abuse.

Irene also refers frequently to her new and crucial perception of the role played in her life by a "Higher Power." This part of the recovery process is often difficult. Many people resent the idea of a Higher Power as an intrusion of religion. Irene is a good example; her initial rejection of the Higher Power concept originated in her own religious upbringing. Once she was able to separate it from her past, and see it as a form of transcendent love and acceptance, she could draw on it for strength. Irene feels that this spiritual growth is an integral part of her recovery.

In summary, Irene's story provides a good basis for approaching the subject of eating disorders. It is a clear demonstration of two concepts critical to understanding the disease: (1) that an eating disorder is a disease in the classic sense in that it has a set of defined symptoms, the etiology of which is beyond the control of the individual; and (2) food can be, and is, abused like many other substances that are currently recognized in the field of substance abuse treatment.

Her story also demonstrates two concepts critical to understanding recovery: (1) effective treatment is based on a behavior approach— changing the eating behavior, rather than understanding the "underlying causes" of the eating behavior; and (2) effective treatment is not a diet. The emphasis is not on losing weight, the emphasis is on changing the eating behavior.

IRENE

"When They Handed Out the Candies, I Was Done First"

One of my earliest memories was of the man next door telling me that I had been the fattest baby in the whole world. I wasn't; I was 7 pounds, 8 ounces or something. I mean, I was a normal weight. I wasn't a huge baby or anything, but they told me I was the fattest baby in the world, so there was an emphasis on that, even when I was little.

Another thing that I find very interesting is that when I went back to my mother to make amends to her and to try to explain my eating disorder, she said she knew it was my dad's fault. Because when I had just come home from the hospital, I was sleeping longer than new-borns normally sleep. I would sleep eight hours at a time, so my father says, "You wake that baby up, and you feed that baby every four hours." So, in essence, when I was only a few weeks old I was force-fed formula too, which is sugar water. I don't know if that could be the beginning of a sensitivity to sugar or whatever; it seems like it might be. Because that overeating has always been there.

When I was little, in preschool, I don't remember being fat. I was sturdy; I was a very sturdy child. But I always remember when they handed out the bag of candies, I was done first. I'd try to get my brother to "let's share," and he would give me some of his. I have great memories of food, of eating a lot. One time my mother went to get some of us at a neighbor's house for lunch. I couldn't have been more than five years old. I went home and I got the lunch. It was two cans of chicken noodle soup with water in them, and I ate the whole thing. I remember kneeling on the stove over the pot of soup. My mother said, "You must have been hungry," and I said, "Well, yes."

I didn't know that there was anything odd about this. I matured very early, so when I was nine or ten, I was put on diets. Everyone else got a popsicle at the beach, and I got juice and diet crackers, which took me years to get over.

I was constantly threatened with the chubette shop. "If you don't stop eating, you will have to go chubette." My mother held it over my head. Chubette was going to be it. And when she remodeled the kitchen, there were locks with keys put on the cookie cabinets, because of me.

I Was the Only One With This Eating Problem

There are nine kids in my family. I'm the second oldest, and all of us were born in twelve years, so it was a very chaotic upbringing. I was the only one in my family with an eating problem. My mother to this day only weighs 114 pounds; she's small. My dad's a little overweight now, but he was a skinny guy. Several of my sisters have gone through 5-pound weight gain things or something, but no, never like me. My mother also served very healthy meals. We would get two vegetables. We had vitamins; we had whole-wheat bread. There were cookies around, but I was the only one who was overdoing it.

I do have one brother who is a drug addict and alcoholic, who has been through treatment and that kind of thing. My dad, I believe, is a maintaining alcoholic. He's not a drunk, but he has two drinks every day and checks out of the family life. My mother is the most compulsive personality I have ever seen in my entire life. She does not overeat or take drugs, but she is controlling—it's incredible. I think we could safely say it was a dysfunctional family.

But mostly it's my brother and I who have manifested compulsion to an extreme degree. With my brother, when he was about 18, it became a matter of jail or treatment; the drugs got to be that bad. But I was the only one with this eating problem.

My mother's biggest thing was the bullying, to try to get me to stop eating. She told me at one point, she would cut her throat if she ate the way I did. And I remember her touching my arms and saying, "It's just so sad." She would wait always until she got me in the department store, in the dressing room. It was a real setup: "We're going to buy new clothes," "I'm so happy," and then, "Isn't it gross that you're so fat?"

Total Denial

In eighth grade I weighed 136 pounds and I was 5 feet, 3 inches tall. So I was not grossly obese, but I was big for a twelve-year-old girl. One time a therapist asked me about my body, how I felt about it while I was growing up and everything. And I had no problem with it, because I was in total denial that I was chubby. I thought that I was 10 or 15 pounds overweight and I just let it be like that. I was always pretending to go on a diet. "I can eat twenty, no, not twenty but a whole package of cupcakes, because I will go on a diet tomorrow," which of course I didn't do. And, I remember I stole money from my mother's purse—anything to get candy—and being totally humiliated when my mother told the neighbors not to give me any more cookies.

I remember once I went on a diet because I wanted to make sure I got a part in a play my senior year in high school. I ate nothing for breakfast, for lunch I had a thing of yogurt, and for dinner I had a can of green beans and sometimes one scoop of vanilla ice cream. Any kind of dieting I did, there was total insanity in it. I got down to 145 pounds, which for me was skinny. I did get the part in the play.

There was always the thing about the weight; it was always the thing. I had all the binge buddies, friends who would eat with me. I finally noticed the difference in our eating. My best friend and I would make chocolate chip cookies and sit up all night eating them. The next morning I'd plow right into breakfast. She would stop then, and maybe not eat 'til dinner time. So, my weight was escalating.

I also had all those little rationalizations: "So long as I can fit in normal-size clothes, I can't really be fat." "So long as I don't have to go to a fat-lady store, I can't possibly be that fat." So there was so much denial. When I got to college—oh, this was great: I got mono my first week at school, and I had bad diarrhea. The doctor said, "Eat gravy and potatoes and thick soups to get rid of your diarrhea." Well, I was off and running then. I mean, I was off and running. I don't know how much weight I put on, because I was in total denial. I think I weighed about 165 my senior year before I went on this diet. I used to always say, before I got abstinent, "I wasn't really fat in high school, I wasn't fat." But when I went back to look at pictures, I was fat. There is no way around it. I was fat.

Looking Back, I Had Friends but We Didn't Talk

I was very popular. The thing was, I did have dates. I had a date for every dance that came along, and I had a boyfriend my senior year. In fact, I had two boys who wanted to go out with me. I was popular. I was on the student council. I had a very big mouth, did a lot of screaming, a lot of attention-getting behavior. I was wild. I never did anything so wild that I'd get arrested, but I was always the one with the nerf ball while the nun had her back turned, throwing it out in the hall, all that kind of stuff. I had a real big mouth, I really mouthed off a lot.

I was very close to my friend, Susan. I did not get along well with my mother at all. We had big screaming fights; we even hit each other sometimes. She would say that was all right though, because we would fight and get it over with, not hold grudges. So I loved my friend Susan's house, because it was very quiet, and she had a canopy bed, and they had special knickknacks around. Having eight brothers and sisters, I didn't have much of my own stuff. I didn't even have my own personal hairbrush until I went away to college. People went in my drawers and took my stuff. It was chaotic, very chaotic. So I always loved Susan and her house. I wanted to live there. I couldn't understand why she hated her dad so much until a few years later, when we were in college, she told me he was an alcoholic. I was shocked, because I thought her dad was the greatest guy, because he would drive us around and buy us stuff. She had grown up listening to the screaming and the yelling and the affairs and so on. But in high school we never communicated that way. So, although she was my closest friend ever, we didn't really talk. But I probably told her more than I told anybody else.

My Perfect Sister

I had a lot of friends. I did reasonably well in school, too. I managed to go to a good college. But it was hard to feel any sense of accomplishment because my older sister was incredibly perfect, incredible. She was very thin, big boobs, lots of boyfriends, had long blonde hair down to here.

She was head of the art club. She was number one in her class. I don't know if my mother was really saying it, but I always heard, "Why can't you be smart like your sister?" I passed French one year because the senile old nun thought I was my sister, and even though I would get a D on a test she would give me a B.

My father was very fond of my older sister too. Then, in 1971, she ran away from home. This was very big rebelling, and she was gone for a long time. My parents didn't know where she was. I remember thinking to myself, "I'll make this up to my parents. I will never let this happen to them."

Too Much Responsibility Too Early

I had a lot of responsibility, too. I thought it was normal when I was seventeen for my parents to go away and leave me with my seven younger brothers and sisters to take care of. I did a good job. I knew how to do all those things; I was very responsible. By the time I was seventeen, I knew I was perfectly capable of running a household with seven people younger than me. I knew how to do all the grocery shopping and all the cooking.

Keeping up this responsible front caused a very big trauma when I went away to college. My father didn't want to take the time off work to drive me to the airport; I was supposed to get on the plane with my trunk, and then figure out by myself where I was going. I grew up in a small town in the east; it wasn't like I was Miss Cosmopolitan or something. I had to cry. I had to go through, "I can't do it. No, I can't do it." I had to beg my father, "Please take me," because I realized I couldn't handle it alone. It was hard, because on the surface it seemed like I could do everything, have everything together, take care of myself, do everything that I needed to do.

I think also, I've learned a lot about this in Al-Anon. I was taught very early, "Don't need anything, don't ask for anything." It was always, "What do you want now?" I was always told that my emotions were out of control, "You must learn to control these emotions," and I remember hearing constantly, "That's ridiculous." Whenever I voiced a feeling or a concern, I heard, "That's ridiculous." It was a typical family, no one ever talked about anything. My mother was pretty nuts, and my father wasn't there, because he was out working. That was his job, to get the money, so he just wasn't there. Sometimes I think I'm letting my father off the hook, because I don't have any bad memories of him. That's because I don't have any memories, good or bad—he just wasn't there. So mom took the rap for most of the chaos and everything.

College—Eating Whenever I Wanted

When I got to college, I was fulfilling some of my dreams of eating whenever I wanted. Also, I started drinking and getting high. I had gotten drunk a little bit in high school, always abusing it from the very first moment. There was no such thing as just having a beer. Instead I would drink a bottle of wine and throw up. I mean, that was my usual thing. So, in college, I kind of went a little bit nuts with all that kind of stuff. I remember thinking after a while that this marijuana thing was out of control. I really didn't feel like I was getting much done, because of marijuana.

So, I stopped the drugs for a while. I didn't get high, but my girlfriend and I had binge buddies in the dorm, and now my eating was out of control. I tried to vomit, because my girlfriend said, "We'll just throw up," but I couldn't. I put my finger in my throat, and blood came up, and I got scared. They said it was probably just a blood vessel in my throat and wasn't dangerous. But, luckily, I got scared, because I did not get into vomiting, although I thought that that was just the best idea. "Throw it up, no problem." Well, I remember my friend and I decided to be on diets, and so what we'd do is, we'd get together all this "diet food" and then get high and eat it all. We still both managed to lose 20 pounds or something, while just getting high and eating stuff like american cheese, because when you're young it's much easier to lose weight. So, off and on through college, I dieted, or didn't diet.

Then I met my husband-to-be, I met him at a thin time. He was older than I was, and he was out of school, so he had money. We got into going to different restaurants. As a student, although my parents didn't keep me impoverished or anything, you eat your meals in the dorm and you go to on-campus stuff. So when I got to go out to restaurants, I really started eating a lot. I think I had what they call a "setpoint." I'd always end up about 165 pounds. I'd lose 20 pounds but end up back there.

After College—The Actress

I think when it really got bad for me is when I left school. I left my boyfriend. I was going to be Miss Independent, and I was going to move to New York City and be an actress. Talk about totally naive—I had no clue. I honestly thought that I would go there and they would put me on Broadway. I had just turned twenty-one, because I started school early. I was a year young for my class. After I graduated, I went home, saved up money, worked for the summer, and my girlfriend and I moved to New York. It was a very traumatic experience for me. I got a job as a salesgirl and that was going great until I quit it, because I had to be an actress. But then I didn't have the courage to go on any auditions. I was so unprepared. Basically, what I did is, I sat around eating and I was unemployed for a while. The millions of things you can eat, I ate.

Then my mother started getting on my back, "You're getting so fat." "You're getting so fat." At times, I wouldn't see her for two weeks, and I might have gained 10 pounds in the two weeks if my eating was serious enough. Then I would diet for a little while and lose the 10 pounds and then go right back to it. Finally my mother— she is ever so helpful and ever on the spot—came up with a liquid diet.

This was in 1974, or somewhere around there. Well, I was too embarrassed to go to the drugstore to get it myself, so my mother went for me. I know it's incredible, but I was just having liquid meals twice a day. I started out eating a normal dinner, like chicken and a salad, but eventually I decided I could lose weight even more quickly by just having a carrot for dinner along with the liquid. By this time, I had such terrible diarrhea that, literally, the food was going right through me. But that didn't matter, because I was losing weight. I made no attempt to evaluate that diet medically. My mother just said, "It'll work. The druggist told me that it's really good."

The reason I stopped it is, I was coming down in the elevator one day with my father and I got so dizzy I thought I was going to pass out on the street in New York City. There was obviously something wrong in having horrible diarrhea and eating one carrot and two liquid meals a day. I could have died from palpitations. My electrolyte balance was gone. So my father said, "Why don't you go get something to eat at the coffee shop." Well, I was off and running again, eating again.

Escalation of the Disease

About that time, my money ran out in New York, so I moved back to the city where I had gone to college. I told everyone it was because all my friends there were working, and some of them were, but mostly I came back to my boyfriend, because I could be taken care of there. And from then on my eating went steadily out of control. I got bigger and bigger and bigger, it was a really bad time for me. I was gaining weight at a terrific rate. I was working a totally insane job; working about eighty hours a week for no money.

Before this, a lot of my binging had consisted of eating too much of everything. But, at this point, my girlfriend introduced me to candy and a drink which is a cross between chocolate milk and soda. When you switch from eating things like spaghetti and bread to eating candy and sugar water, the weight comes on fast. I didn't know quite how much I weighed. At this time I decided to marry my husband. I got married, squeezing into a size-20 wedding dress. I was getting fatter and fatter; my job was more and more insane.

I was doing public relations for theater companies, so we had to hustle everything for free. We had no help. It was complete insanity, but the theater was everything. Also, I believed these people would really appreciate me when they saw how much I did for them, which of course didn't work out that way. By this time I had a pre-ulcerous condition in my stomach, so I knew that something was wrong. After I got married, I decided to get rid of this job. My mother started once again about, "Got to lose weight; got to lose weight."

When I finally went to my first diet class, I weighed 225 pounds. I lived in terror of someone asking me to go for a walk or something, because my feet were so swollen. I had trouble walking and didn't want to wear pants because I had this grand illusion that I looked thinner in skirts—as if at 225 you're going to hide anything! But I kept this grand illusion that if I didn't wear pants, it didn't show. When I think back now, it's kind of embarrassing. I had one or two jumpers and different shirts. I had a hard time putting on pantyhose, so I mostly just wore knee highs.

My husband didn't pressure me about the weight. He used to ask me if I was sure that it was good for me. The issue of sexuality and that kind of thing never really seemed to come up. Whether he was thinking about it or not, I don't know, but he was worried about me because I was gaining so much weight.

Now, I had no concept that I was gaining this much weight and looked this bad. I thought that they were making the dresses differently this year. I said that to myself; it wasn't me getting fatter, it was that the styles had changed and they were cutting skirts "thinner." I had no idea that my husband was an alcoholic, and so we were busy enabling one another to eat, drink, and all this kind of stuff. The thing about the alcohol for me was that I would stop drinking if I was afraid there would not be enough room for food. Like when I went out for Mexican food, I didn't have beer because beer filled you up too much—there wouldn't be enough room for food.

Starvation Dieting

Then my mother intervened again and said, "You've got to go on a diet, you have to do something." So just to pacify her, I picked a diet class out of the newspaper. I went there, signed up, and I was going to be the queen of the diet class. They made a deal with my husband that he wouldn't give me any food. Because, in this class, you eat everything out of little boxes, and the only thing you get to eat that's real is a salad. I managed to cheat on that, too: once my brother-in-law was watching me measure a cup of salad. I was jamming the lettuce into the cup, and he said, "It's a cup of salad before you put it through the food processor." I used to do things like order pizza at night, eat half of it, put it in the garbage, say I wouldn't eat any more, and take it out of the garbage and eat it. I did all those sneaky things. I would go into the bakery and say, "I'm having a party so I need ten of these," as if this woman in the bakery would care; she's glad I'm buying bakery goods.

I went to the diet club, to be the queen. I realized there was something wrong, though, when I would sit across the table from my husband and cry and beg him to go get me popcorn. I would beg him. I remember thinking, "You know something is really wrong with an adult woman who's crying for popcorn." I had the concept that there was something wrong even at that point.

I did the diet and I lost 75 to 85 pounds. I went through their accusing me of cheating, because I plateaued for a couple weeks. I was crying hysterically, because they loved me when I lost weight, and now they didn't.

I developed, once again, incredible diarrhea. I was afraid to leave the house, because sometimes I would be walking down the street and I would have to hold still just to try and hold it in, because I was going to embarrass myself. I talked to them. I saw their doctor. They changed the diet, worked it around, and finally the nurse, whom I had gotten very friendly with, whispered to me, "You've got to go see your own doctor; this shouldn't be like this." Well, I didn't have my own doctor, but my brother-in-law had a doctor, who turned out to be a wonderful woman doctor who was very understanding. Also at this time, my grandmother was in intensive care in the hospital and my sister's husband had left her with two children. I ended up being the family's savior, of course, driving to the hospital, helping my sister, trying to get her husband back, and so on. I had said to this doctor, I didn't know if maybe the diarrhea could have been emotionally based, because standing over my grandmother's death bed I felt like I was going to pass out. So the doctor very sensibly said to me, "Well, perhaps it does have to do with what you have been eating, because when you don't eat it you feel better." I thought, "Oh, there's a flash." She also told me that the diet class had approached her to be their doctor, but she turned them down because it was dangerous. She suggested that I try something more sensible, or something that was better. So I did that, and in another diet class a real miracle happened. The first week, I went and I ate four ice cream bars and I still lost three pounds. I ended up losing altogether 95 pounds.

All I Did Was Eat All Day

But as soon as I was back on regular food, I was cheating. Pretty soon, I can't remember the exact amount of time, I stopped going to my new diet class and I was doing things like, can you save all your potatoes for one day? Can you save three baked potatoes and have three at one meal? Can you save the three beers you are allowed to have for one day? I was able to stay pretty much the same weight for about six months or so, and then it went wacko, out of control. I mean I was so bad I was doing nothing but eating, eating gross things, cookie dough, anything, anything that I could get. I would go to the grocery store embarrassed, wearing a hat and sunglasses because of the amount of food that I was buying. And then I would throw half the wrappers out the window of the car.

As I drove home, I would stop at every fast-food place and go through every drive-through. I was gaining the weight back really quick. Then I would go on an all-protein diet, and I'd have seven eggs for breakfast. I even tried to go back to my first class because they allegedly had a new fiber diet, but within ten minutes I was so nervous about it, or didn't want to do it or whatever, I had a stomachache, I could only do it for one day. I even went to a health spa where I sat there crying in front of this woman. I don't know why she didn't send me to a psychiatrist instead of letting me charge $500 on my credit card (which I never got back). As soon as I got home from there, I knew this was wrong.

I think that's when the big awareness came that there was really something wrong with me, because being in the first diet class had been the hardest thing I've ever done. I said, "I'll never do this again, I'll never be fat again," and yet here I was. The eating was much worse than it had ever been, because it was so concentrated. Basically, all I did was eat all day. It's too bad they invented those cookies with the batter already made, because I would put half in the oven and eat the other half. It was bizarre.

I Just Wanted to Be Dead

Also at that time I knew I was emotionally disturbed, because I was suicidal. I didn't think I could kill myself, but I'd find myself thinking that reverse bus lanes were a good idea because I could accidentally step in front of the bus and no one would know it wasn't an accident. I would wake up crying to my husband, telling him I just wanted to be dead. He and I have talked about it now, and he says he didn't know what to do. He had no idea what to do, and it was just getting worse and worse. My clothes didn't fit from one day to another, and I really didn't know what I would do with myself.

This is funny: when I was at my most skinny, right after the first class, I went and had dinner with an old college roommate, who had been a binge buddy. She was saying, "Oh, you look so great." I looked fabulous. I had dyed my hair platinum blonde, and I just couldn't have looked cuter. We went to this place and we were talking about diets. She said that she "tried that Overeaters Anonymous, but those people were too screwed up." Now that must have stayed with me, because a year and a half later I knew I was very screwed up. I knew there was something wrong with me, but it took me a long time to call OA. I remember calling OA as I'm making brownies and telling myself, "They aren't going to answer the phone, so forget it. Besides, I have to eat these brownies." I think everybody goes through this. Finally, I underlined OA's number in the phone book. And maybe a month or two later, I called.

OA—"I Eat Like a Dog"

I called because I knew that I was messed up. Everyone else I knew could eat one piece of cake. It seemed to be only me who had to eat the whole cake. I knew there was something much more wrong with me than just eating. I also knew that there was something wrong with doing something as hard as being in the first diet club and not sticking with it. So finally I called, got an OA meeting, and said, "Now I have to go."

I only weighed about 185 then, so I'd only gained back about 45 pounds. I figured I was pretty svelte. I thought everyone there would weigh about 700 and have to have five chairs underneath them. I do remember wearing clothes that I thought I looked fat in. I was rather defiant. When I walked in, there was only one lady fatter than me, and everyone was trying to be nice to me, which of course I could not handle. I was crying, and I was a mess. Some people came to me, and they sat there and listened very intellectually, but I was falling apart. This one girl tried to hug me. I said, "Get away from me." I couldn't stand the Twelve Steps; I couldn't make amends. I said, "I have no defects of character." I was telling them how I couldn't do that, how I didn't believe in God, because just one week before I had decided there was no God. I was raised Catholic, and I was surely going to hell.

The thing that made me come back was the woman who told her story and said, "I eat like a dog." She talked about putting cigarette butts on pizza, throwing it in the garbage, then taking the butts off and eating it anyway. She talked about tearing the packages up into little pieces and flushing them down the toilet so no one would see what she ate. And I, honest to God, thought I was the only one who did that, and, oh, it was such a relief to me. Then she said, and this made sense to me too, that when she was on a diet and had gone to the second diet club, where lettuce was "free," she would get a big bowl and put three heads of lettuce in it and eat that. I was so gratified to hear about someone else doing this kind of thing, because at that diet club, someone would always say, "I ate two brownies last night, isn't that terrible?" And I'd be thinking, "Two? Let's get real, let's talk two dozen, let's talk major." Because when I was in that bad phase of gaining all that weight, I would make up pounds of spaghetti and sit in front of the TV crying into the spaghetti with all the lights out asking, "What is wrong with me?"

I Could Come Back

At OA, I knew there was something for me. This man came up to me—and I know him now, and he is so funny—he says I was the angriest person he had ever seen come in the door. But that night he came up to me and said, "Can you come back next week?" I started crying all over again, because for once someone had asked me something I could do. I couldn't be on the diet, there was no way. I could not be abstinent. I could not call anyone; I was not capable of all that. But I could come back. I could come back the next week. And I did come back the next week. I remember the week after that I was going to be out of town, so I told everyone, "Well, I'm going to be out of town, so you'll know where I am," thinking that they cared, and they said, "Well, that's good to know." Somebody asked me what my abstinence was like, and I immediately created a diet for myself, where I could eat whatever I wanted so long as it was under 1200 calories, and I called this abstinence.

I remember too, they said, "Ask God to help you." Now I lived around the corner from a donut shop, which is a great place for a compulsive eater. I remember driving home from meetings saying, "God, please help me drive past the donut shop," and I did. That was a miracle, because I had never done that before. I didn't have a sponsor. I didn't call anyone. I only went to one meeting a week, but I think I wasn't eating sugar. We weren't supposed to eat sugar, so I did that.

Grateful to Be Alive

I was suicidal when I walked into OA, but within two weeks I went to a meeting at Thanksgiving and I was grateful to be alive. It was like an immediate change. I remember Thanksgiving. There was a woman who had been going to my Tuesday night meeting, and I arrived when she did, so we went in together, and I remember crying to her and saying, "I don't want to be dead anymore." There was a big change there.

But it wasn't perfection. On Christmas Eve I went to the bakery to buy cookies for my nieces and nephews. There were shapes of trees and wreaths and stuff, and they broke on the way home, so I decided I'd have to eat them. That Christmas, I was eating so fast and so furiously, even before the food got on the table, that I didn't have to make myself vomit, I vomited spontaneously. I had to put myself to bed, and then I was off and running again.

I had lost 10 pounds, which I immediately gained back. When I went to the meetings, I would say, "Well, you know I'm a compulsive overeater, so I can't help myself, but even though I'm still eating like crazy it's all getting better," which is the grand deception. I think that things do get better. Obviously, once you're not alone and you're with someone you're going to feel better, even if you're still practicing. But I went into that great deception of, "Look, I'm still eating like a dog, but my life is getting so much better, my relationships are a miracle," which wasn't really true at all. But I kept going to my meetings, and it started to change.

I Could Tell God That I Was Angry

At one meeting a guest speaker talked about how she also had lost a lot of weight. Well now, a lot of the people in the meetings I went to either hadn't lost weight or didn't have a lot to lose, and, I'm sorry, I had trouble relating to people with 6 pounds to lose. To me anything under 160 was unacceptable. If you could wear size 14 pants that was fine. We all had different levels of what would be okay. This woman talked about how, first of all, she had lost 150 pounds or something. She was normal size now and she'd been abstinent for a long time. Then she talked about how she hated God, and how her sponsor said, "You have to pray," so her prayer was, "Okay, screw you, God." She told God she was angry at Him because He had never made her thin. For the first time, that opened the door for me to think. Having been raised with religious beliefs, I thought you had to have your chapel veil on and your uniform straight and your hands folded to be good enough to pray, and for the first time I realized that if I was angry at God, maybe that was okay. I didn't have to be Mother Teresa to qualify for prayer. I could tell God that I was livid, that I was foaming at the mouth I was so angry.

A Sponsor and a Food Plan

Then another woman came in late for the meeting, and she happened to sit in the seat next to me. Well, it turns out that she had also lost a lot of weight, 120 pounds or something, and she still had weight to lose. She said that she would be dead if it wasn't for this program, and I knew that I was going to be dead, that there was not much time left for me. At the rate I was going, I knew it was either insanity, death, or getting better. I began crying again, hysterically crying, sitting next to her, and I turned to her at the break and I said, "Would you please be my sponsor?" I don't know where the courage came from. She said, "I don't have time, but you call me tomorrow." I said, "What time?" She said, "nine o'clock," so I called her at nine o'clock. She said she guessed she could be my sponsor, but what did I want from a sponsor? "I don't know," I said. I was crying, I was a basket case. She said, "Did you pick out a food plan?" They used to have a food plan, a pamphlet with several different food plans in it. Well, I chose the one with the most food. For youths it was; for growing youths. So I started, and I called in my food every day. I would call in my food and I would be crying.

She took me to a Big Book meeting, which helped me to begin. Now I was going to two meetings a week, which helped me to understand a little bit more of what the program was about. I don't know if she realized it, but I used to write in my calendar, "Call at ten o'clock," and watch the clock for the seconds to go around, because that was really the only thing that was getting me through. She told me to ask God for help in the morning, say thank you at night, call her, and eat my abstinent meals. My meals were my priority. If my husband suggested we go some place different, I'd say, "We can't. We must eat this meal right now." My total focus was on abstinence. I was eating large meals, I was eating starch, vegetable, fruit, protein, a glass of milk at every meal. I wasn't eating anything between my meals or anything I didn't commit. I was eating healthy food. I think just not eating all that trash must have made my body feel better. And knowing that there was someone that I could call, that this wasn't a secret any more—it was like I was a new person, almost right away.

A Small Measure of Reality

Eventually I began to talk about my feelings or what I felt like. After I had been abstinent four or five months, it was time to do the Fourth Step. This is how out of touch I was: my sponsor told me to write down all the people I had a bad feeling about, so I said, "I think, my family." I had maintained that I had a perfect childhood, that it was just so much fun having eight brothers and sisters, that we just shared all the time, that it was wonderful, that I was so self-sufficient. Now I had maintained this entire fantasy for a long time, but now I said to her, "I think maybe I hate my mother, and I think maybe my family wasn't so perfect." And my sponsor said, "Is there anything else?" But I didn't know anything else; that was all to come. It was like the beginning of becoming in touch with some kind of reality, some small measure of reality.

Abstinence—Freedom from the Bondage of Compulsive Eating

The first year I remember mostly being abstinent. I did start to lose weight, and basically what has happened with my abstinence over the course of time is that for a while things will be okay and honest, and then I will start to feel bad about my food. Even though it's my regular committed food I'll realize, "Wait a minute, there's something that's not right." So there have been many adjustments and many changes in my abstinence. Some foods would be okay for a while, and then wouldn't be okay, and now they're okay again. I used to have a very strict food plan. Now that I'll have been abstinent four years in February, it's okay if I want fruit at breakfast and fruit at lunch. It's a little bit looser, but I feel okay with it.

I was reading a book the other night, and it was talking about levels of truth. As you grow as a person, what's true to you may go through a change, and then something else will be true. And I really believe in my first year of the program that my life was managed by someone or something. Now, looking back after four years, I thank God I had the honeymoon, because if I had known what was going to be asked of me, to give up and to go through and to look at myself—I might not have made it.

I think that I didn't really feel a significant change until I started being abstinent. I think that you can go to OA meetings and keep on eating and develop friends and feel better. I think that you feel better not being alone. But I think that the real promise of the program, which is freedom from the bondage of compulsive overeating, comes with abstinence. In my compulsion days, I would get up in the morning and think about what I was going to eat, and then what I was going to eat next. My weekend was spent reading the back of the local magazine, picking out which restaurants I would go to and what I could eat at each one so that I could have room at the next one.

Now that I'm free from the compulsion, I enjoy my food, and I think "Oh, it would be nice to have that left over," or "I'd really like turkey for lunch," or something, but I don't think about food all day long.

It was very hard to lose the compulsion. I started to lose it some time in the first year. It would come back, but I would just hang in there. I was in such bad shape that I would have done anything to stay abstinent, anything. If they had said, "Eat dog crap," I would have done it, if that's what it took. Because I was at bottom. I remember seeing a commercial for chocolate chip cookies on TV and starting to cry because I felt I would never have them again. But hard as abstinence was sometimes, I did not want to go back, that was one thing I knew for sure. I was terrified of that, so I held on to my abstinence. "If this goes, I'm gone." It was so serious. I often ate my abstinent food very compulsively, but that was okay, that was okay then. But mostly, the food compulsion probably was lifted in a major way almost from the beginning. I think that was because of the horrible shape I was in.

"Is a Life Worth This Penny Candy?"

I had a very revealing experince not long ago. I was sponsoring a woman who had just come out of treatment, and we went to see an AA priest give a talk at an AA meeting. As we're driving home in the car, she says to me, "I have to tell you, I've been binging, and all this stuff is still up in my room." So, I said, "Okay," and I went into her apartment and she gave me the stuff. I didn't want to throw it in the trash can outside, because I thought, she'll go in there and get it, which is what I would have done. So I brought it home. I went into my apartment, and I thought my husband can take it to work, give it to the people there. When I put it on the counter, I saw that it was a bunch of penny candy and trash. We're not talking Viennese pastry or some quality item—we're talking crap. I said, "Is this worth a life? Is a life worth this penny candy and this crap?" It isn't. And my husband, who has now gained some understanding about the program, said, "No, it isn't." It's really kind of sad.

Cleaning Up the Past

I remember, too, when I had my year's abstinence, I didn't want it. I felt it was too much responsibility. I felt like, "Oh, God, they're going to expect me to keep doing this." The other big thing that happened after I was abstinent for about a year and a half was that I would suddenly start crying. I got very unhappy; my honeymoon was over. I would be driving down the street and I would burst out crying. And all of a sudden, my relationship with my sponsor became very bizarre. What had, in essence, happened, was I had transferred onto her, the way you would in therapy. My relationship with my mother and everything I had avoided through eating and never dealt with, which was my whole, entire, chaotic upbringing, was beginning to come out with my sponsor. But I had to be clean a year and a half before I began to realize that there was something in the past that needed cleaning up. And at that time I did go into therapy, and that has helped me a lot, this cleaning of the past, and understanding my family and coming into reality on that. I have been able to ask, What really went on and what really is going on? It's been a lot of help in recovery.

There Were Too Many Expectations

I was raised with a very controlling mother who, after the fact, always said, "If you'd only done it like this." I was raised to be self-reliant, and I was told that I could do or be anything—the American girl with all the advantages. I was blonde and blue-eyed, but I should have been thin. I was smart and perky and funny, and I had all the advantages, so why couldn't I achieve everything? I got sent to the best schools, I got sent to Europe. Why couldn't I just be thin and be happy and do everything right? I was a girl who was supposed to be perfect.

One more thing, the denial in my home was incredible. I remember what my father used to say to my brother. The kid is completely high and looks a total mess, and my father would say, "When you go out tonight, will you behave like a Christian gentleman?" My brother would go, "Yes, dad." And dad says, "None of those funny cigarettes now," meaning marijuana. My brother would go, "Oh, no, dad, no." The next thing we find out, he's a drug dealer, but it's like my father thought because he had said, "Don't do this," that my brother wouldn't. The denial is so strong.

That's what my mother did, too. She would get us all together and tell us how things were. If something happened in the neighborhood, she'd say, "You're not to play with those children, because those children's mother does blah, blah, blah, and we know that is wrong, right?" We'd all go, "Yes, mother," and we'd leave the room. It was mother's version of reality, her little propaganda.

I remember her saying things like, "Well, you'll go away to college and you'll be this and that." When I moved to New York, I remember thinking to myself, after she built this wonderful picture, "What does she think this is, a TV sitcom or something?" My mother told us what we were supposed to think, not what was really true. She told me what my father was like, what this one was like, what that one really wanted, and I remember saying, "That's right, Mom." Sometimes I think I had to eat to sedate myself in order not to ask. "What is wrong with this picture? There's something that's not quite right here."

Denial of Reality—No More

It's funny too, because in both my mother's and father's families, I don't think anyone drank that I could see or there was evidence of. But you don't need to have alcoholism there to have some denial of reality. I think there were major denials of reality all the way around.

You know it's another interesting thing, my mother-in-law is really totally out of reality, too. She wants us to be one big happy family, even though my father-in-law is completely insane. It's all this off-the-wall stuff. Two of her children were institutionalized for mental illness while growing up, and the third, my husband, was in therapy because he couldn't cope and dropped out of school. She tells stories about her husband's mother, how she dominated the entire family and did all these horrible things and made them all go on vacations together and all this. But then she'll sit there and say, "Next year, we'll all go on vacation together, it will be so much fun, just like it was." And it wasn't fun, it never was. Then she'll say to me, "Where else could you have a good time except in a big family like this?" They've all had six drinks, they're all tense, and no one is having a good time. But that, "We are a happy family!" myth continues.

Family: Relating and Detaching

I relate differently to my family now. Most of my therapy issues arise from my mother, and that's a difficult one for me. I do relate to her differently now in being able to detach a little bit. I have a long, long way to go with that, but I have extracted myself a lot from my family's day-to-day insanity and affairs.

Right now, my mother is engineering a family feud. It's one of these things that's designed to have several people not speak to one another until one of them dies. She's engineering this. I am not becoming involved, I will not talk to anyone in the family about it. If they all want to hate each other and fight, fine, but I'm not taking sides.

I've been able to see, too, that certain members of my family want to stay in their diseases. When my brother went into treatment for drugs and alcohol, my mother refused to participate. The family was supposed to go into family therapy, but she's going to have absolutely no part of that, and my father couldn't go because my mother wouldn't let him.

I said, "Dad, how old are you, fifty-eight? What do you mean, she won't let you? You don't own a charge card? You can't get on a plane and go?" (My brother was in treatment far away, near where he had been going to school.) My mother said, "Your brother will have to get well on his own." Anyway, when he came back, the whole family was a little bit on eggshells—whatever he needs, don't upset him, and all this kind of stuff. He went into treatment just a little bit after I came to OA. He's a lot younger than I; I think he is twenty-four. My mother thought it was really good when he made it a year in the program. They all went to the anniversary, and she says, "It's so funny, these people stand around and say, 'Hi, I'm Phil, I'm an alcoholic.'" But, with my brother, I think that they are finally realizing the miracle here, that this kid could have very well been dead. So, sometimes it's kind of hard when I've explained to them about having an eating disorder, and it doesn't get the same respect.

In fact, my mother had a friend whose kid was 300 pounds; she said, "What's that diet group you went to that's finally worked for you?" But even though I've explained it, it doesn't get the same kind of respect. My disease just isn't taken as seriously. To them, it's simply now that I'm pretty I can be happy—just because I'm thin and pretty. They have no idea of how much deeper it goes.

Al-Anon and OA are helping me with my family, my relationships—more than just my eating disorder. I always had trouble with relationships, with my bosses and people in the outside world. I never had a job before that I didn't quit in a huff, and now I am actually able to talk to my boss, because I also teach, work things out, learn to take care of myself bit by bit. Also I realize that most of my emotional involvement is inappropriate, that these things are not to be taken so personally. That's been really tremendous.

Closer to My Sister

One of my sisters goes to Al-Anon now, too. She was at school, and she knew something was wrong, and she didn't know where to go or what to do. So she went to an Al-Anon meeting, because she said, "Maybe I can go there, because my brother's an alcoholic." She said this woman told her her story, and even though she couldn't really see alcoholism, the meetings have really been helping her. So I feel that I can talk to her. When I go to visit her, she's there, and we have a camaraderie. My weight, my disease, showed I was obviously in need of some kind of help. My brother was obviously in need of some kind of help. My older sister is carrying all the same things around, and I suggested she might want to see a therapist. She said, "No, I have to get better on my own." Because she doesn't drink and because she doesn't overeat or do drugs, she doesn't have any place to go. So maybe, in a way, I was lucky to have some kind of symptom to force me to get help. I mean there was something really wrong, and we all knew it.

The thing about families is hard, because it eventually comes to the fact that sometimes they don't want to get well. So, there has to be a big letting go. It's hard because, even though they are sick relationships, they're my only family. So it's hard, I think I am involved in that process now, of letting go.

Marriage—A Growth Process

There has been a lot of change in my marriage, and a lot of that has been very difficult. When I first started changing, he was scared; he was really scared. He thought I might be in a cult or something. After my first meeting I came home to him and I said, "I have a disease, I'm really sick, and I have to go to bed now." I was literally putting myself to bed; I needed elbow straws and stuff. I was crying so hard coming home from the first meeting, I missed traffic lights. It's been hard; there were times when I didn't know if my marriage would last, even before I realized there was alcoholism. He would say to me, "Do you still love me?" and I almost wouldn't know what to say. At one point he came up to me, and he said, "I'm afraid you're going to change so much that you won't want to be with me anymore." I had to say to him, "I don't want that to happen, but I don't know if it will happen." Getting through all that has been a real growth process.

I think the really big change for me in my relationship with my husband has been my going to Al-Anon. He's another alcoholic, like my dad. He goes to work, doesn't get drunk too much, but there is always alcohol present.

I went to Al-Anon for six months and things got better right away, because they always do when you go to Al-Anon and you learn not to be a maniac. As I improved, our home improved, so I thought I didn't need it anymore, and then I had to go back. I've been going very faithfully for over a year now, and it's helped me so much. I was not the type of Al-Anon woman who is submissive to her husband. I was mouthing off, screaming, yelling, breaking dishes,—you know, histrionics. As I improved and stopped that and got off his back about things that didn't matter, he's taken me seriously on things that do matter. So what I feel like right now is that we have a relationship which is a negotiation. I don't know how it will turn out, but I am very hopeful that it will work out. I used to threaten all the time. "I'm leaving, I'm getting a divorce," I said that every twenty minutes. I don't say that any more, because I'm not ready to walk away from the relationship now. It's a scary place to be, but I think with the help of Al-Anon I am negotiating.

A few weeks ago we were talking about how I used to behave. He told me that he was scared and he didn't know what to do with me. He thought I was going to kill myself. He really didn't want to leave the house. We also talked about the way I used to treat him, constantly haranguing him. It was a real codependency. It was especially hard when I was changing and he would accuse me of acting the same old way. If I didn't comment and I let it go, he would do anything he could to trigger my old reaction of going berserk, to get those patterns back into play. So it's been difficult that way. I feel that I've grown a lot, and he's grown a lot, and the relationship is growing. He does talk about whether he is an alcoholic or not. I did all that— degrading him, telling him, screaming at him—I did all that stuff. I went through all the things you're not supposed to do. I did all of them before I started doing the things you're supposed to do. The idea that he is an alcoholic is no longer under the blanket; it's out in the open. He did start in therapy, and I don't know if that is good or bad. I don't know if it's a crutch that will make him think that everything is going to be okay, or if it's something that will really help him to more awareness. I don't know.

Today: No Compulsive Decisions

I don't think about abstinence for eternity. I still sometimes have separation anxiety about certain food. I don't like it when dinner is over. I will always have to deal with food in my life. I will always. It's not as bad as it was, but when I'm going on vacation, I must plan ahead what I'm going to eat. Also, now I'm much better about knowing whether a decision is a compulsive decision or not. My husband and I are going to England. So if the plane is delayed twelve hours, and it's three o'clock in the morning and we're on the plane, and I might not get anything to eat for the next seven hours, what will I do? This kind of thing would have thrown me into a trauma before. I would have had to make an intercontinental phone call.

But now I can say, "Okay, what seems sensible? What seems like the right thing to do?" And I can say to my husband, "You know what, I think I'll have the protein, the starch, and the vegetable now. Then when we get there, I'll get some fruit juice or something." You know, I can make a decision for myself that is not a compulsive one, but about being healthy and doing what my body needs. In my first two years of abstinence, I could not make a decision like that; I was not capable. It would have thrown me into complete and utter trauma to have to do that on my own.

I have to think about these things. I have to make a plan for myself. It's not like it was at the start, "I must have chicken and green beans," but I must still pay attention to what I'm doing. Let's say I'm invited for dinner at someone's house at eight o'clock. That means we probably won't eat dinner until 8:45, so I must plan my food so that I can have my snack at 5:30. My abstinence doesn't keep me from enjoying life, but I must pay attention to this; I can't just let it go.

I think it gets better the longer I'm abstinent. When I first started, when I went to a dinner party, I would have my own dinner in my purse, in case they served something that made me feel uncomfortable or that I couldn't eat.

A Problem with Feeling Good

I'll tell you, I'm scared of relapse. I still sometimes have dreams. I had a dream last night that I started eating. It was so graphic. I remember just what the cookies looked like. They were like peanut butter cookies, and I would put chocolate on them or something, and I remember chewing and then thinking, "You can't have this, you're abstinent," and taking them out of my mouth. I still have dreams like that. Also, I still ask, "Why me? Why not her over there?" I am still working on this all the time. One of the big problems I'm dealing with, and I never understood this before, is about feeling good. I've been learning a lot about myself in the past two months. All of sudden, a lot of things in therapy have just clicked, and a lot of things in my spiritual life are beginning to click, and I say, "I'm feeling like a healthy person—watch out."

I tell myself, "Don't get cocky, because you'll lose abstinence." But then again, is God going to punish me for feeling good? I mean, I'm still going to all my meetings and calling my sponsor and eating my abstinent meals. It's hard, getting over expecting trouble, because how many times do you say, "I thought everything was going fine," then, boom! So, in a way, I think I'll wait for the "boom."

I Can Find Something Wrong with Me, but Still Be Okay

I think the biggest thing that has been helping me lately is this: For the first time in my life I can find something wrong with me, but still be okay. Always before I had to be perfect, I had to have all these defects licked, and my abstinence perfect, to go on living for today. Today I can say, "You know what, I still have a real problem with letting go of my family, and I still have a real problem with manipulation and control, and I'm very judgmental, and I still have procrastination, and all these other defects, but that's okay. I can work on them and continue to grow." I have self-acceptance now, whereas before I was either a horrible piece of dirt—or you were a stupid idiot if you didn't see the marvelous and wonderfulness of me. All the usual grandiose stuff to cover up my real inadequacies.

Accepting Myself

I've acquired a new acceptance of my body. I always had to be 125 or I wasn't a good person, but my body seems to rest very comfortably around 135. So I finally decided, instead of never achieving my goal weight, maybe I should raise my goal weight to 135, which I maintain with no problem and with ease. I couldn't exercise, either, until just recently. I joined health clubs and I couldn't go. I had been, in my bad days, exercising compulsively and then saying, "I will not go to the bakery. I will not go. I will not go." And walking right into it. It just happened to be near the "Y." Now I'm beginning to be able to exercise a little bit, not in a compulsive manner. But I also have to give myself a break. I'm not a bad person because I don't have cardiovascular fitness. I let myself do what I can do.

I have a male friend who's in the same business I'm in. He's always romping, stomping; seeing this person and that person; getting his resume out and so on. I can't live like that, I can't. Not that I don't work hard or don't want to achieve; I do. But I no longer miss romping and stomping and getting everything done. I still have terrible defects with controlling and manipulation that I never even knew were there. If you had told me that I was a manipulator four years ago, I would have said, "I am not." I think abstinence lets me see myself more clearly. I've had to make discoveries about how manipulative I am, how controlling I am, how I am a compulsive talker. It has been very embarrassing, but I've had to look at all these defects all the time.

One of the Miracles of the Program

I think that abstinence is so important because I had to let go of something. If I don't let go, I don't know how a Higher Power or God could help me. And, at the start, I did not believe in God. I really felt beaten before I ever started. The only way I really got to believe in God is that I didn't have to eat a gallon and a half of ice cream with chocolate sauce over it. On a daily basis, with help from God, I did not have to eat like that any more. I don't think there is any such thing as perfect abstinence. I think perfect abstinence is impossible. But it is possible to have food in its proper place in your life. I think, just from that, I can say there is a God. And slowly I can begin to develop a spiritual relationship.

I still feel like a total infant in terms of finding spiritual relationships. It was more like "God help me" whenever I was in trouble. But now I'm coming to a newer understanding of what a Higher Power is and what it really can do in my life. In one of the meditation books it said, "I may make mistakes, but I am not mistaken." And, I think I'm just beginning now to be able to stop feeling that I am a big tragic mistake, an awful human being, a terrible person, unless I achieve all these great things. I may or may not be talented, but I'm still a good person. I may or may not end up with a successful marriage, but that doesn't make me bad. Getting over this feeling of "badness" that I had, which we could call low self-esteen, or poor image, or whatever, is one of the miracles of the program.

Preface to Dave

Where does a "big appetite" end and an eating disorder begin? Can a person maintain two compulsions—such as alcohol and food—and be successfully treated for one of them without addressing the other?

Dave knew he was an alcoholic when he went into treatment. He was surprised and a bit skeptical when he was told he also had an eating disorder. But he went along with the treatment program because he was told that he would not be able to treat his alcoholism successfully unless he also treated his eating disorder.

Looking back, Dave is grateful that he picked, by sheer luck, a treatment program that dealt with cross-addiction. "I enjoy eating, and I enjoyed it a lot more then, and I could easily see myself dealing with the alcohol withdrawal by eating." He had no awareness, at the time, that eating was as much of a compulsion for him as alcohol was. "I think the only reason I would have even considered the fact that I may have had an eating disorder was because I was so overweight. And yet, again, I didn't feel like I 'fit in' to an eating disorder program."

Dave's story brings out some of the differences between men and women in the way they experience an eating disorder. In our society, men have much greater latitude in acceptable body types and in eating behavior. Unfortunately, women are still valued more for their looks than for anything else, placing enormous stress on the individual for her appearance. And the esthetic standard for women is unrealistic, to say the least, resulting in a continuous perception on the part of the average woman that her body is somehow "wrong." This provides a ready foundation for a body obsession and the onset of starve-or-binge behavior.

On the other hand, our society values men for a much wider range of human attributes, placing less stress on the body. In addition, a big appetite is tolerated and even admired in men as "masculine." As a result, men aren't as inclined to the body-obsession that is so characteristic of the eating disorder in women, and may not experience starve-or-binge behavior to the same degree that women do.

Dave's case is representative of an eating disorder experienced by a man. He was uncomfortable with his weight, but it was not the major preoccupation in his life. His self-worth was not predicated upon being thin. In contrast to Irene, he was not constantly trying to stop eating, or caught in a starve-or-binge cycle of diet and weight gain. He was almost able to perceive his eating as conforming to a socially accepted male model of "the big eater." His size was a clue that something was wrong. But again, he felt it was not that much of a problem, given the greater social tolerance of obesity in men.

As a result, it was difficult for Dave to fit into the eating disorder program. As one of only two men in the group, he felt totally out of place. His experience was not as dramatic as that of the women in the group. Not until a male guest speaker came to his Overeaters Anonymous group and identified his own compulsive eating behavior did Dave clearly see where he fit in.

"I find myself turning toward food to suppress a feeling or to make myself feel better, but it hasn't been to the point where I couldn't stop myself." This is important for people who simply do not experience the dramatic symptoms of someone like Irene, but for whom eating and weight are experienced as constant problems. The problem still requires the same treatment, and will respond to that treatment. Diets are not enough, and only contribute to the problem.

The other part of Dave's story that is especially significant is his alcoholism. It is common for an eating disorder to be concurrent with another addiction. One can conceive of a basic disease—addiction—presenting itself through many different substances, one of which is food.

Other elements of Dave's story that are highly representative are his coming to terms with his essential isolation and the development, for the first time, of meaningful relationships; his attempts to understand his family, and his new spiritual awareness. Dave exemplifies the beginnings of recovery and the faith that keeps it going.

DAVE

I was always overweight, I can remember being a child—maybe six, seven years old—and I remember really wanting to eat a lot. But I never really considered it to be an addiction. I didn't know, of course, at such a young age. As a matter of fact, I didn't even know it when I went into treatment. I went into treatment for alcoholism. I was very sick. I was near death. It was fortunate for me that I picked the treatment center where I went. I didn't really pick it; it just happened to be the first phone number in the book under alcohol treatment and I came across it. When I went in for my evaluation and they asked me some questions, they said, "We think you might have an eating disorder." At the time I was 320 pounds. I certainly was not going to argue with them.

Difficult to Admit to an Eating Disorder

When I went in for the evaluation, I had no place else to turn. I had absolutely nothing to lose, and I was tremendously terrified. So whatever they said, I was willing to agree with, and they put me on the eating disorder team. To be quite honest, I'm just really now, after a year and a half, dealing with food in a way that I think a lot of the people that I was in treatment with were dealing with it when they first went into treatment.

I would say the majority, the vast majority of the people that were in treatment with me, were there for the food. A lot of them had gone through other treatments for alcohol or drug addiction, never looking at the food, and one just leads right into the other sooner or later. You know without getting food under control, you're going to drink or use drugs again. And, it was difficult for me to admit to the fact that I had an eating disorder.

Admitting that I had an eating disorder was harder than facing up to alcoholism. I knew I was an alcoholic. I was drinking almost a fifth of vodka a night for about eight months, and prior to that, ever since I can remember, I always drank more than anyone else. So I kind of had an idea that I had a drinking problem, long before I went into treatment. Things had gotten so bad with my family, my wife finally left and took our son. I did not have a job for eight months, and never made any attempt to look for a job, although I was saying, "Yes, I'm looking for one." My life was literally falling apart about me, and I knew that was because of alcohol. It was just a matter of feeling totally worthless and hopeless. I tried to stop drinking a few times. I could not go a day without a drink.

I Continually Thought of Eating After I Thought of Drinking

Most of my eating, most of my compulsive eating, took place after I had started drinking. My pattern generally was to start drinking around nine o'clock at night, after my wife had gone to bed. Once I started drinking, then I started eating, and I would eat large amounts, like two or three sandwiches, a pizza, a whole frozen pizza, or something. Not anything like I've heard in meetings or in treatment, but certainly more than any other person would do.

My trigger foods were snack-type foods; salty, snack-type foods— pretzels and peanuts. Once I started, I couldn't stop with those, and it would just lead into other things. Sandwiches, I loved sandwiches. Get a loaf of french bread and make a sandwich. But again, that was all after I'd started drinking, or well on the way to however far I was going to go drinking for a particular evening. A lot of that is really foggy in my mind.

I can't pinpoint a bottom, as far as the food went, other than the fact that I was so overweight. And, I was extremely embarrassed about that, and very, very self-conscious. I felt that any time I stepped outside the front door, the whole world was looking at me. And when I used to walk into a room, I used to look around at the furniture and see which furniture would be easiest to get in and out of. It was just like there were two people inside me. There was one who was kind of worried about what was going on, but he was certainly secondary. And there was the person who needed to be in control, the person who needed to have the drink, and he was dominant for a very long time.

So it's very difficult, as I said, for me to pinpoint any bottoms or any particular outstanding incidents in my mind as far as food goes, other than the fact that I continually thought of eating right after I thought of drinking. We would be invited out to dinner to my parents' house, or my in-laws' house, and they would always, whatever was left over, they would always pack it up for us. As we were sitting there eating dinner, I would be thinking, "Oh, this roast beef is going to make a nice sandwich later." Or I would eat maybe not quite as much as everyone else, because I knew that later on I would be able to eat more, and I didn't want to make a spectacle of myself.

And my weight, my size, were such that I knew everybody there was concerned about it. Some people, my father especially, would say, "You know, you really have got to start losing some weight," and I'd say, "Yeah, Dad." Again, it was the two people, with one saying, "Let's just get out of here. We'll go home and take care of what we really want to do." Today, it's a lot easier for me to see the compulsive overeating in my own life and how it was in the past, and I feel it, I feel it all the time.

Overweight Child

As a child, I know that it seemed to me that I was always eating something, all the time. I always had something in my pocket. I'd find a quarter or something on the street and friends would say, "Hey, let's go to a movie," and I'd say, "Oh no, I'd rather go out and get a cupcake or something."

I remember one of the most embarrassing things that happened to me growing up as a kid. I think it was in seventh grade. We were putting on a Christmas play, and they asked me to be Santa Claus. I went to a Catholic school, and the nuns said, "Yes, and we won't need any padding." I was very overweight in grade school. Actually I went into high school overweight. I can't even guess how much, maybe 20, 30, 40 pounds.

I went to an all-boys high school and I took a lot of abuse in high school for my size. So the summer between freshman and sophomore year, I went on a very strict diet—water and a lot of protein—and I lost a lot of weight. I started playing a lot of sports, and it seemed that through the remainder of my high school years it wasn't much of a problem keeping the weight off, or even eating.

I started to drink in high school, but I don't think it was anything different from anybody else—you know, maybe a beer after a dance or splitting a bottle of wine between three or four guys. I don't recall it as being anything unusual. Basically I'm a very, I don't know what the word is, a very "scared" person I suppose. When I turned twenty-one and it was legal for me to start drinking, I started to go into bars. I was terrified to do that before I was twenty-one. And, when it was legal for me, I think that's when I really started to abuse the alcohol. Bringing it home, sneaking bottles in, stuff like that.

Old World Family

My father was an alcoholic. My mother was, I would guess, the textbook enabler, certainly seeing it, but not saying anything. I don't recall very many fights. I can remember arguments, but they didn't seem to be unusual. My father was not a violent man. I loved them both, but they're both gone now; they passed away. My dad died of a heart attack, and I'm sure that it was in conjunction with his drinking.

They weren't very strict parents. I can remember always, though, trying to get my dad to spend time with me. It was very, very important to me. He wasn't around a lot. He worked the afternoon shift in a factory, and then he bought a tavern with one of his partners and he was gone a lot. I saw him from in the morning until about noon, when he left to go to the tavern. Then he worked at the tavern until closing. So we didn't see him a lot; we didn't do a lot of family things together. I think my mom basically brought the kids up, on a day-to-day basis.

My mom was a very loving woman, very compassionate—maybe almost too loving and too compassionate. I can remember that for any given problem that I had, I could've gone to Mom and she would have taken care of it. I lived at home until I got married, when I was twenty-five. There were a lot of times when I was obviously drunk, and in the middle of the day, rather unusual times for somebody to be drinking. I would tell Mom that I was just tired, and she would say, "That's okay. Just go back to bed."

If something was wrong, she would fix it, and if she couldn't fix it, then she would pat me on the head and say, "That's okay, Mom's here. Don't worry about it. Your Mom's here; she'll take care of you."

My parents were just first generation over from eastern Europe, Lithuanian background. My grandfather lived with us until he passed away. In my family it was a case of "the man is right." The woman just does what the man says, and, once you're married, that's it, you're married. No matter what happens, you're stuck for good.

Marriage—We Never Talked

So, that's the way my mother was brought up, and that's the kind of household I was brought up in, and I carried it into my marriage. Fortunately, (today I could say fortunately) my wife, now my ex-wife (we were divorced last December), was not of the same upbringing, and finally she just had enough and said, "This is it," and it was quite a shock to me. I mean, I thought we were married, and that's it.

When I met her, I was drinking heavily, but not anywhere near how it was toward the end of my drinking. I would say I was drinking probably every day, but it was only maybe a couple of drinks. And she also liked to enjoy herself and have a few drinks. So it was a pretty good match at that time, but then she just kind of stopped. After our son was born, she stopped drinking. She would have a glass of wine every now and then, but you know, when you're an alcoholic you can't stop at any time, so I just kind of continued when she stopped.

We were married eight years, and in that time my drinking progressed a lot more because I was more independent. I worked the night shift. My wife worked the day shift. So I had a lot of free time. We didn't see each other much. That was one of the complaints. We never talked, either.

In the evening, early, we spent time together. I would be coming home from work at eight in the morning, and she would be leaving. Then she would get home about five, and we would spend the evening together and I would go to work. So generally the pattern was for me to come home from work, say "good morning" as we passed in the hallway, and then I would drink and also eat. I can remember doing a lot of two TV dinners or buying a box of fried chicken. I think fried chicken was probably my main food, my main drug of choice, if that's how you want to put it. I would buy a ten-piece box of fried chicken, or frozen fried chicken, and cook it and eat eight pieces, but leave the two wings or something. I wouldn't want to finish it because if I ate all ten pieces, then there was something wrong, so I would leave the wings.

I practiced a lot of my addictions and compulsions alone. It went on that way for quite a while, until my wife became pregnant, and somehow or other that rang a bell in my head. I tried to straighten out for a while, and I did. I cut back to drinking only on weekends, and not alcoholic drinking, but social drinking. But that didn't last very long.

Birth of My Son: I Was Still Drunk from the Night Before

I can remember the morning that our son was born. The night before I had drunk very heavily, and we were driving to the hospital that morning, and it was fortunate that we made it. My wife was so nervous and in a lot of pain, so I don't know if she noticed it or not, but I was still drunk when we drove to the hospital. I stayed with her during the birth, and as things progressed, I think I sobered up rather quickly. But that morning, when she woke me up and she said, "My water bag broke, and I think we have to go to the hospital," I somehow tried to convince her that it wasn't time. That's how bad it was. But we got rolling and as we were driving to the hospital, I think it was kind of a forced sobering, very sobering, effect. It was kind of like when the policeman pulls you over because the tail light is out, and you drive very carefully after that.

When we got to the hospital, I remember the admitting nurse commenting that I was very cool, very calm. You could have said I was anesthetized. But it was a very long day, and I remember going through a lot of physical pain sobering up. Then later, when we brought our son home, he developed a severe case of jaundice. We had some relatives over one Sunday. Again I was drinking, and we were watching the football game, and the ladies were coddling the baby, and someone commented on how yellow he was. As a matter of fact, the first few comments were rather humorous, "Oh, he's suntanned," stuff like that. But I guess the maternal instinct took over, and we brought him to the window in the sunlight, and he was very yellow. So we called the doctor, and he said, "You've got to get him in immediately." It was a real scary time. We brought him in. He needed a transfusion from his mom, and our doctor said that we were very fortunate, that there was a very good chance that he could have suffered severe brain damage. I don't know that much about it, although at the time it was all explained to me a hundred times. He was in intensive care over at the hospital for a week in their neonatal unit, and every night I went home and got drunk after that—something that I'm not real proud of, but that's the way it was. I was very sick. I can't remember much about it.

I would go through periods of maybe a week trying not to drink, and then start drinking. I held a job during all this time; I was working at a hotel. I was the housekeeping manager.

Progression of the Addictions

I was progressing in my eating, too. I was continually putting on weight, and again it was hard to see me eating at that point. It was real hard for me to see. I had this big black spot in my mind, and that was my drinking, and I knew that I had a problem with drinking. But I always told myself that I could stop any time I wanted to. It took me a long time to find out that I couldn't stop when I wanted to. I told myself, "Well I can always get help when I want to." But it took my wife saying, "I want a divorce," and leaving one morning, for me to realize that now was the time. The alcohol was the black spot, and I was not able to see anything besides that.

When my wife left, it was at a point in my life when I could have made two decisions. I could either continue with what I was doing, using alcohol and using food, or I could get help, or try to get help. By the grace of God, He gave me just a taste of hope—something that I hadn't felt in many years. I was very fortunate. I had a very close friend whom I went over to see the morning that my wife left. I was expecting a lot of sympathy from him, a lot of, "Oh, I'm sorry," "You can stay here," and "Anything we can do?" That's what I wanted, but he listened to what I had to say, and got up and got the phone book, and said, "You need help. You need a lot of help." And we called the treatment center.

Treatment: I Couldn't Relate to the Eating Disorder

When I checked in, they asked me a lot of questions about eating patterns. When did I eat? Of course they asked a lot of questions about self-induced vomiting and all that, which is what most people associate with an eating disorder.

For a long time that kind of blocked me from accepting the fact that I did have an eating disorder. I certainly couldn't relate to the people who did not want to eat at all for fear of gaining weight. I couldn't relate to the people who would eat and then vomit intentionally, or the people who use the diuretics or laxatives. It was hard for me to actually admit that I had binged. I had "overeaten." I guess in my mind there was a line between "overeating" and "binging." I had never gone out and spent ten, fifteen, twenty dollars for any kind of snack food or anything. It was explained to me, and I would agree that it was more of a grazing type of eating, constantly, all the time. Once in a while something would trigger, and then I would eat more than I really wanted to eat or physically felt that I could hold. I can remember eating two dinners relatively close, or at least one full dinner and then eating some more even though I was full. I would be physically full, but just continue to eat.

They put me in the eating disorder program, and I felt out of place. I felt out of place with the other eating disorder people because I was there to deal with my alcoholism. I thought that was my primary addiction, and I couldn't relate.

I would sit through the groups thinking, "No, that's not me. This is not me. I don't know what they're talking about." This one here threw out some food and ten minutes later was going in the garbage to pick it up. And, frankly, at that point, that disgusted me. I thought, "My God, these people are sick. I know I'm sick, but boy are they sick." As a matter of fact, I would have to say in the beginning I didn't even accept that they were sick. I had a disgust. I mean, sure, alcohol is an addiction; it's a problem. Drugs are an addiction, a problem. But food? Food is food.

I Tried to Keep an Open Mind—
Because I Could See Results

It was difficult for me to go to the therapy group sessions because eighty percent of the talk was about food. But gradually I could see that the people I was in treatment with were sincere. The thought even ran through my mind (of course there were a lot of crazy thoughts in those early days of treatment) that some of the people were actually on the payroll of the treatment center, trying some kind of shock therapy!

I didn't even know what the words "anorexia" or "bulimia" meant. "Eating disorder"—I didn't know what that was. They said, "You have an eating disorder." And I thought in my mind, "Yeah, sure, I'm 120 pounds overweight. Sure, okay, I'll agree, that's fine." "And we're going to put you on the Z Team." "Yeah, that's fine, Y Team, Z Team, I don't care, whatever, just help me as much as you can." I knew I belonged there from the time I walked in the door. I knew that was where I belonged, but not with the food, only with the alcohol. I never really fought what they tried to get across to me. I really tried to remain as open-minded as possible, with a mind that was really messed up and abused for quite a while. But almost immediately, on the food plan, I could see the results, I was losing weight, and I said, "This is great."

We Were the Only Two Males on the Team

We had in-house OA meetings, and then we had to go out to certain OA meetings, once or twice every week. I was not feeling part of the team, not being able to relate. There was myself and another guy on the team, and then there were fifteen, sixteen, seventeen females. Thank goodness there was another guy on the team, otherwise I don't know whether I would have talked to anybody.

At those first OA meetings that I went to, I was the only male there, or one of two in a room of twenty or thirty females. It was very intimidating to say the least. I felt like I could have walked in there with a helmet with a red light flashing on top. It was really hard for me to talk. It's a miracle for me to be sitting here right now and talking about it. A year and half ago, I wouldn't answer the phone. I wouldn't answer the door. I wouldn't talk to my wife when she wanted to talk. I wouldn't talk to anybody. I was just afraid. I was just terrified of what, I don't know, maybe of what I might hear. It took me two or three weeks in alcoholism treatment before I would even talk voluntarily. I was confronted a few times, and I talked as little as possible. And then for me to go from that to an OA meeting where there were all these ladies—it took me quite a while to even say anything.

Difficulty Talking About Himself

It was the first time in my life when I was expected to talk about myself on a personal level. From childhood, right from birth, I don't ever recall having any real, deep discussions with my parents, with my sisters, with anyone. It was, "How are you?" "I'm fine." That was it.

Marriage was the same thing. Either my wife or I, mostly it was I, would have a bad day. It's fairly obvious when somebody is not quite in the right frame of mind, and she would say, "Had a bad day?" and I would say, "Yes, I don't want to talk about it." And that was it; that was the end of it.

The treatment was the first time I had to talk about myself. I think it was scary, not only getting over the initial embarrassment of thinking that my problems were the worst, but also, for me to talk about myself, I was actually talking about somebody that I knew less about than anyone else.

"This Is It!"

I remember when I started feeling more comfortable with OA. I went to one in-house OA meeting and there was a male speaker. He looked very well, but at the beginning of the meeting he passed around some pictures of what he used to look like. At that point, that's what I looked like. Then he described pretty much what I could remember about my eating patterns. He didn't mention the words binge, or anorexia, or vomiting, or any of that. It was just eating and really enjoying eating. He was like me.

I think that's the first time I heard the term "graze," and I can remember coming out of that meeting feeling just wonderful. It was like, "This is it."

While I was in treatment I became very spiritual, and I relied a lot on God. God and I had many conversations, mainly my asking for help and trying to understand. At that point it was about the eating disorder. As I said, there was no question in my mind about the alcoholism. I mean that was cut and dried, black and white. But I think probably the only reason I would have even considered the fact that I may have had an eating disorder was because I was so overweight. And yet, again, I didn't feel like I fit in, so I kept praying for some type of insight, some type of explanation, and at that meeting, I felt, "This is clear to me now." If this person has an eating disorder, then so do I. Because I have what he has. And, I think it helped probably quite a bit that he was a male. I may have heard the same story from a female, but I think there was still that wall there of immediate nonrelating.

Today, My Eating Disorder is Clear

I walked out of that meeting, and I really felt good. I felt like I belonged there. I guess it would be really nice to say, "Ever since that moment, I've known that I have an eating disorder," but that's not true. Sometimes I even doubt the fact that I'm an alcoholic. But, today, for me, my eating disorder, my compulsive overeating, is very clear. I can see it so much more because in the early months of recovery there are a lot of stressful times. There were a lot of times when I used to turn to drinking and then, secondarily, to eating. I really had nothing to turn to other than what I had learned in treatment—talking, going to meetings, using your sponsor, using your friends. I surrounded myself with program people. There have been many occasions when something has come up, even not very serious, and I could be sitting on the couch one minute, and the next minute I find myself standing in the middle of the kitchen, looking around. The compulsion is still there. I mean, food is a drug. It's an addiction, and I have it.

Grateful for Treatment of Cross-Addiction

I'm more grateful than anything else that I ended up in treatment for both addictions because there are so many places that just treat alcoholism, and I don't know whether another treatment would have been as successful as far as the alcoholism goes.

I could see myself going to a treatment center where they are trying to get alcoholics and addicts back on some type of healthy eating patterns and encouraging eating, and I would abuse it. I enjoy eating, and I enjoyed it a lot more then, and I could easily see myself dealing with alcohol withdrawal by eating.

The way I see it, it's a system of trade-offs. If you are a compulsive person, you're a compulsive person. I could easily have substituted a lot more food for the alcohol had I not gone through the eating disorder treatment. I have friends also that just went in for the alcoholism, and they put on a lot of weight.

An alcoholic with an eating disorder will go into treatment, stop drinking, come out, still be eating compulsively, and still practicing compulsive behavior. Eventually it will lead, can lead, and easily does lead back to drinking again.

I have a very close friend who is anorexic, and she is very thin. We talk a lot about disorders, and one of the first questions we ask each other is, how is your food going? She is still having a hard time with it. We were in treatment together.

It has seemed easier for me to deal with the food then it has been for her. So I don't know. Sometimes I find myself thinking, "Well maybe I'm just borderline, maybe I don't belong at all. Maybe it was the alcohol. Maybe it was just the sugar." But then she says, "You know, I think it's probably better for you because you can see the results." I think that had a major effect on me, that I could see tangible results. I was eating what I should—not all the time. I certainly wasn't perfect by any means. But I was basically sticking to a food plan, and I continued to lose weight. So, with me, the program works.

Today I am a gratefully recovering alcoholic and compulsive overeater. When I first heard that term, I thought those people were nuts to say that. But I've had an opportunity, whether it was by my choice or not, to look at myself, to recognize things that need to be worked on. And not only to be shown what to look for, but to give me a feeling inside that when I recognize that behavior, even if I choose not to act on it, there's something like a bell inside that says, "This is wrong." I can no longer just ignore things about myself. I can't consciously be dishonest.

Before, if I didn't want to go somewhere, rather than tell the person I don't want to go there, I would say, "I'm having a problem with my car." I've done that and other things, but after it's over, I don't feel good. I'm not saying that it's a gnawing, agonizing pain, but it's there. Not many people have that opportunity. I see a lot of people within my life that are not in the program, that could use some of the things that I learned. A lot of people just don't choose to look at themselves, and you can go through your whole life like that. I think there are a lot of people walking around who are alcoholic or have an eating disorder, if you will, and may never take a drink. They have the characteristics and the personality, the perfectionism, the ego, the need to be right, refusing to look at any negative characteristics. Just blind. I can see that in myself, and I'm really grateful that I can.

Family and Friends

Before I went into treatment, I had no relationships with people. I had one very dear friend, whom I isolated myself from. I had no relationship with my wife—my ex-wife. My closest relationship with another human being was with my son. He was five when I went into treatment. Today, it's another world. I've replaced my relationship with food and alcohol with relationships with other people.

One of the biggest regrets that I have, probably discounting the fact that I'm not as perfect as I want to be, is that I do not have an opportunity, at least for maybe an hour or so, to talk with my mom and my dad. And that's something I'm really having a hard time dealing with. I can only think of what kind of impression, or what kind of appearance, I may have given my parents in their last year. I knew I was very sick, and now I know how sick I really was. I don't recall any specific incident, but I'm sure I must have done some rather crazy things. I would just be so grateful, even if it would be just to say, "Hey, look at me today. I'm doing okay, and I wanted you to know that."

A couple of weeks ago, I sat down and I talked about this with some friends. They suggested that although I can't talk to them, maybe I could write them a letter, go to the cemetery and leave it there, or whatever. I tried doing that, and I probably got about three or four lines into the letter and I absolutely broke down. I started crying. It was really good for me, because I find it very difficult to cry, to express that kind of emotion. Probably that was the first time that I cried in a long time. Since I went into treatment, I probably can count on one hand the times that I've cried, and the majority of those would have been alone. I can remember crying once in front of the group, in therapy, and almost crying three or four times in the company of one or more of the people, but that's something that I wish would come a little bit easier, I really do.

Yes, I wish I could speak to my parents. There's a point in everybody's program where they want to fix the world. I've even thought maybe, had things been different, had there been time, maybe I could have helped my dad a little bit, even my mom. I can only imagine the kind of emotional thing that she had gone through, very stiff upper lip, "nothing wrong." My mom had stomach cancer while I was still living at home. I have three sisters. The two younger sisters and I were still living at home. She was going for chemotherapy, and we never knew it. She and dad left at eight o'clock in the morning, came back about eleven, yet we never knew, and this went on for five or six months. I was in my late teens, early twenties, very much not seeing what was immediately around me. But also, she must have gone to great lengths to hide it, I guess so as not to worry the kids. I didn't know.

I Can Help My Son

You know, I can see that in my son, who's now seven. He refuses to comment any further than, "Everything's fine," and I know everything is not fine. How can it be fine? I mean, we used to live together and now we don't. I see him on alternate weekends. I can see in him a lot of alcoholic characteristics. That's another thing that I'm very grateful for, not only for what I've learned myself, but for the information as to what to look for.

I kind of subscribe to the belief that we all have some type of purpose on earth, whatever that may be. For what I've been through, and I don't mean to sound like a martyr by any stretch, but maybe, just maybe I may be able to help somebody else. And I have a good opportunity with my son.

I Guess It Was a Good Day

Part of the treatment program was to get you to start feeling better about yourself, to stop feeling like such a schmuck. As I said, I was very self-conscious about my size, about my being overweight, and when I came out of treatment, I felt good about myself, because I had lost maybe 20 to 25 pounds. It wasn't hard; it wasn't a diet. I never thought of it as a diet. As a matter of fact, there were some meals when I felt quite full, and yet I was losing weight. Of course, one of the goals of the treatment is not to be concerned with your weight, but to be concerned with the food and what it's doing to you. And, if you follow your food plan, your weight will be where it should be. It may not be what you think it should be in your mind. But, it will be where your body should be, and that was happening to me. I mean, it was actual, physical evidence, something solid, something concrete I could see, as opposed to measuring my progress by something that's going on up here in my head. Do I feel better about myself today? Yes. Do I want to take a drink today? No. Do I want to overeat today? No. Well, I guess it was a good day.

Preface to Jennifer

*Y*ou can't ask why, you just have to accept," says Jennifer of her eating illness. The foundation of her recovery is acceptance. Although Jennifer is deeply introspective and ponders the reasons why, she does not predicate her recovery upon knowing why.

Like Irene's and Dave's, Jennifer's story is a clear demonstration of how the successful treatment of an eating disorder is focused on changing the behavior rather than talking away the highly disputed and largely theoretical causes of her behavior. Psychology abounds with conflicting theories of what causes an eating disorder, and equally conflicting treatment modalities. The common thread throughout the successful treatments presented in this book is that they were based on changing the behavior with group support systems and Twelve Step programs. This does not exclude, however, the need for individual therapy after the eating disorder sufferer has attained a period of abstinence and has been recovering for at least six months to one year, or longer.

Jennifer, like Irene and Dave, grew up in a family in which denial was the standard response to problems. With abstinence she is able to see how she had used eating as a coping mechanism, a "quick fix" to avoid the pain she had been taught to deny. She feels that she grew up without learning how to meet her needs appropriately, or, even worse, unable to recognize her needs for fear that they were "too big." As a result, like Irene, Jennifer became a caretaker, a people-pleaser, because she thought, "if I take, you might not like me, because I might need too much." A distinction should be drawn between the obligatory caretaker and a healthy person who, having met his or her needs, really has something to give. Jennifer found, in recovery, the joy of real giving as opposed to fearful people-pleasing. A recurring theme throughout this book, one of the benefits of the group support provided by successful treatment and Overeaters Anonymous, is that the individual does learn to recognize her needs and meet them within the context of the group.

But for some individuals, problems such as incest, sexual abuse, and alcoholism in the family or a family history of mental illness may require more intense individual therapy. Jennifer was an incest victim, sexually abused by her brother. The problems with "neediness" were thus complicated by a history of abuse within her family system. After achieving abstinence, she experienced extreme symptoms of anxiety and depression requiring careful treatment with antidepressants and individual therapy. It is not unusual for problems to surface once the "drug" (food) has been withdrawn. In Jennifer's case, they required more extensive treatment.

Jennifer is sensitive to the many ways in which the "cycle of addiction" manifests itself in her life. As she says, "The compulsions are more subtle now." She finds that with men she looks for the "quick fix" or that she'll become compulsive about makeup or clothes. The difference in her life now is that she is aware of it and does not allow it to dominate her behavior.

Coming to terms with her family, her feelings, her past, Jennifer struggles to emerge not only from the bondage of her eating disorder, but from the whole destructive complex of behavior associated with it. She experiences the joys of new, honest friendships and the fun of acting out her adolescence at last. She is in awe of the new spiritual dimension in her life and the strength she derives from it. In the end, she sums up her present position succinctly, "I can see another way to be, and I'm getting there."

JENNIFER

● ————————————————————

Six years ago, I weighed about 320 pounds. And I still think I look like that. That's a real problem I'm working on. People tell me all the time that my face doesn't even look the same. It's really something. But I lived like that for such a long time, that's how I think of myself.

It's really going to take some time to change my mental image because I looked that way for about twenty years. I've always been obese. I was never just plump. It was always an extreme amount of weight.

"Why Me?"

It's interesting, because I was premature by about two months, and I weighed about 3 pounds at birth. So they fattened me up. They kept me in the incubator for a while, and they fattened me up. My mom and I have talked about it a little bit. I've questioned her a lot: How did you feed me? What was I like, eating? What kinds of things did you give me? Did you breast-feed me? I questioned a lot, trying to understand what an eating disorder is and where it could start. Is it really manifested in a symptom or allergy in the body, is it genetic, or is it connected to your emotions and your development? I've always wondered about that. It's funny, because when I first joined Overeaters Anonymous, my sponsor was always saying to me, "You can't ask why. You just have to accept." I was always saying "But why? Why? I don't understand. Why me?"

"I Thought I was Going to Die"

I'm twenty-eight. I was 190 pounds in sixth grade, and I never got under 190 pounds until about a year and a half ago. So I was always obese. I mean, in fifth grade I was over 150, and in sixth grade I was

190. My parents sent me to a weight camp for three summers, and I would lose 50 or 60 pounds, but then over that year I would gain the weight I lost plus another 40 pounds. It was always the weight lost, plus. So by seventh and eighth grade I was up to 250 pounds. In high school I was always 240 pounds, and then, my junior year in high school, I got up to about 320. That was my highest weight, and I developed what they called "temporary sugar diabetes."

They called me a juvenile diabetic, and they treated me with insulin. At that point I was so scared, and I was physically in so much pain. I was drinking massive amounts of water and having so much physical discomfort that I felt like I was dying. I was starting to lose weight, and yet I was eating, consuming so much food. They put me on insulin, and I followed their diet. It was so scary. I just followed it, and I lost about 120 pounds in four months, got down to about 190. Then they took me off insulin because my body just started producing the insulin again by itself.

I remember right toward the end, before they took me off insulin, I kept thinking, "Oh, if I take a little more insulin, I can eat more," and I started to calculate how to do that. Well, a normal, healthy person who takes their health seriously or has any sense of self-esteem or self-love wouldn't do that. They wouldn't mess around with medicine, especially something like that where it's so precise. And I remember thinking, "Well I could have peanut-butter-and-jelly sandwiches if I took another unit of insulin." So I started doing that. They took me off insulin, though, and within a year I had gained 60 pounds. I just stopped going to the doctor for a while, and I thought, "Well, I'll know when the symptoms are coming back. I'll know if I'm getting back to that place." Even though I really thought I was going to die, I didn't care.

Abstinence—a Miracle

When I got in OA in 1980, the night I walked into my first meeting, I got a sponsor, and I had obviously bottomed, because from that point on I've been abstinent from sugar and flour and binging. So it's going to be actually six years on Thanksgiving that I haven't eaten between meals. I haven't eaten sugar. I haven't eaten flour. I haven't eaten all my binge foods, and for me it's a miracle. I believe in my heart, when I look at it, that it was a conviction that happened to me when I went to my first OA meeting.

You Have to Admit You Can't Do It

I had heard about OA when I was in college, my junior year. I worked in a nursery school as an intern, and a woman was there. You know, when you're obese, it's funny, people always try to tell you how to lose weight. They've always got these suggestions. And this is the dilemma—everyone said you can do it, you just need self-will. When, actually, the problem requires the opposite approach. You have to admit that you *can't* do it, and when you admit you can't do it, then it happens for you. And I could buy that, because people would come up to me and say, "Try this, and try that," but I couldn't. This one woman came up to me, and said, "Just want to let you know I'm in this great group called Overeaters Anonymous." Then she said, "You can come to a meeting with me sometime." Well, inside I'm thinking, "Leave me alone, I don't want to talk about it, I'm not interested in another thing to help me lose weight." And, I just let it go.

If I Lose Weight, He'll Marry Me

In the fall semester of my senior year, I was drinking a lot of alcohol. I had taken to drinking in college in my sophomore year, and I drank for three years in college. I think I transferred to another substance. Food wasn't enough at that point. I smoked two packs of cigarettes a day. I drank approximately a bottle of wine or a six pack by myself an evening, plus the eating to maintain the 280 pounds, 300 pounds. By the way, since I've been in the program, I've been able to let go of smoking and alcohol for five years.

But I was drinking a lot, and I remember I had met a friend of mine. In high school I had a crush on this guy. I really loved him, but he was an alcoholic, a severe alcoholic, in high school. I had met him when I was home on break that summer, and he had gone through treatment and was going to AA. All our friends used to party together, and he was sober, so he wasn't there. I sought him out, and I found out what was going on. He told me about the program, and we became very close. I think I wanted to be his girlfriend. I was trying to save him, help him. Here I was 300 pounds. I could hardly help myself. And that fall when I went back to school, he called me, and he said, "I've got news for you, there's this program. It's just like my program. It's called Overeaters Anonymous." I thought, "Oh there comes that name again, you know." But I had seen him transformed, and I was so proud of him, plus, in the back of my mind was my sick thinking, "If I get in the program and lose weight, he'll marry me." That's what I thought when I got in the program. So I went to my first meeting, and that night before I went, I was with some friends and I was eating everything I could eat. I mean, I got everything, because this is like the last minute I know I'm going to eat, I'm going to eat everything.

First OA Meeting

On the way to the meeting—it was a Monday night, I'll never forget it—I stopped at a drug store and got a humungous bag of candy and I thought, "I've got to eat this candy before I go to this meeting. I've got to eat them." I remember my car had sidepockets on the door and I remember sticking the bag in the door and just eating them while I was driving there, and I got to the parking lot, still eating.

I went in, and it's a miracle because there was only one woman who showed up at this meeting. She was ten minutes late, and I had said, "If no one comes by ten after eight, I'm out of here. I gave it my shot." This woman walked in, about my age, thin, and she set the whole meeting up. They had these little slogan cards they would put around the table. She put out the *Big Book,* the format, and she sat down and ran this meeting just for me. I thought, "This is incredible, that she cares so much." And we talked about a food plan, and she asked me what I felt about God. Well, I have a handle on God because I come from a Presbyterian family who believe in God, so that's no problem for me, and I committed my food, I wrote it out. Before I left the meeting, I said, "Tomorrow I would eat this and this," and I weighed and measured all my food. And they had a format I followed, one of their suggested food plans, which was very much like any doctor's food plan, where it would have a carbohydrate and fruit and vegetable.

Committed but Scared

It was very balanced, and it worked for me for a long time. It actually had crackers and whole wheat stuff that I'm abstaining from right now until I get to my goal weight, because some things just don't work. But at that time, at 300 pounds, I could eat a lot at each meal and lose a lot of weight. What my sponsor said to me was, the idea is to commit your food so that you don't go to the icebox, open the door, and eat. I said, "You mean I could have cake if I committed it?" She said, "Well, we could talk it over every morning, and if you need to commit a cake in a meal, we'll talk about it, and if you still feel okay by the time we're done talking then that will be part of your food plan." And, of course, I was too humiliated ever to try that.

I called in my food for six months. At Christmas I moved away, and I found meetings in my new city. At that time there weren't a whole lot of people who were abstinent. So I called my food back to my old sponsor for three and a half months.

I was really committed, but I was scared, too. You know, I always had that same feeling, "This is going to end." I finally found a sponsor in my new city, and then I felt like I could go without committing my food long distance every day.

I've been working with the program ever since I've been abstinent. I weigh about 160 right now. I still have got 20—about 25—pounds to the weight I want to be at. Though doctors say, "You're normal now. You know you're lucky you have gotten this low in your weight. You should be satisfied," I don't believe that. I believe I'm normal like anybody else who can weigh 130, 125, 135; that just because I've been obese doesn't mean I can't be healthy and thin. Not skinny, just nice. Even 160 is okay with me. There are people who come in OA at 160 that are bottoming out, flipping out because they are 160, and they're in total chaos about it. I'm 160, and I feel like I'm at the best place I've ever been, but I know I would like to be thinner. I'd like for one day of my life to be 130 pounds.

My Sponsor Gave Me Hope

My first year in the program, even after I moved, when I went to meetings, I would hang out in the back and I would never talk. I just sat in the back. And, at that time they didn't go around the room and talk. You'd have to raise your hand; so I'd never talk. For a year I didn't talk. Now you can't keep me quiet when I go. I'm always out there. I'm always doing stuff. I mean I talk all the time. It's really different, but in those days I didn't. I just held on to my sponsor emotionally and was just so grateful. "Thank you so much for being so nice to me." I was really humbled, I think, by her believing in me.

And I call her still every year on my anniversary. She says call her and let her know I'm still doing it. She hasn't had the same kind of abstinence I've had. She's had a problem with sugar withdrawal throughout the time that I've known her, which is okay. I don't worry about her; I mean I'd love her not to have to do that because it hurts her.

I still can't believe I got what I got, and that she gave me that hope that I could get it. She believed in me, and she told me I was going to be okay. When I would call her up, freaking out, I would say, "Okay, I'm not allowed to eat a candy bar ever again? Are you serious? Now come on, never again?" It seemed like this mass of time. "Never again" just seemed too much.

Emotional Liberation

I felt like I had to cry every day because I never again would eat certain things, and that thought of "never again" just petrified me. Today I don't care. Today it's been lifted, that need or that obsession or that craving. The craving to eat sugar or to eat like that was lifted after about the eighth month. It took a long time. I had to go through that pain of withdrawal. See, I'd never gone that long before on any diet. I never gave myself that chance. With diets you can eat sugar, you know. You could say, "Well, I'll cheat today." So I never got that withdrawal from sugar long enough to see that it was emotionally liberating too. I never got that. I finally woke up one day, and I thought, I'm not on my knees going, "Help me God" so much. I'm just on my knees saying, "God, today you have to help with food," where, in the beginning, I was white-knuckling it. I just did what they told me. I shut up and I listened. I really believe that's why it worked for me, because I knew at that point I couldn't do it alone. And it was life or death for me.

My sponsor was just a wonderful person, she was perfect for me, she was very calm. She was a firm believer in the *Big Book* of Alcoholics Anonymous and the Twelve Steps, and she quoted stuff to me all the time. She'd tell me to read certain Steps, and really gently, very gently, she'd tell me I was a wonderful person, that I deserve to be happy, that I could do this. I had never heard that, you know. She told me that when I was 300 pounds. It wasn't, "When you get to be a certain weight, you'll be okay."

I Would Do Anything; I was Insane

Something she said to me seems almost unbelievable, like a fairy tale. That night of the meeting, she said, "Are you willing to say to me right now that no matter what, you are willing to try to work through this, with an understanding that you may *never* lose your weight? Do you want it that badly? I mean, is the pain that bad? If I were to say to you, 'I'll give you happiness, but you may never be under two hundred pounds,' would you be willing to still work this program?" At that time I said, "I'll do anything. I'm just insane."

When I look back on it, I realize that was where I was. A lot of people come into OA with 10, 15, 20 pounds they can play with. If I only had 20 pounds, I could play with it. I could diet for the rest of my life and be happy. I would have those swings of being depressed at 20 pounds up, but I could also lose it and be happy for six months and then gain it back. But with 150 pounds, it's just different, a different way to be. So for me, my focus was, I was out of my mind. I am a misfit; I don't fit in. I was a size 50 pants. Matter of fact, I have a pair of pants that I've saved—one pair, and I can fit in one leg now!

After I got into the program, I grew out of a lot of friendships. I lost a lot of friends. Well, actually I shouldn't say "lost." I chose to move on. And what was really interesting, being a compulsive eater, one of the manifestations of the disease is people pleasing. Because you want to be accepted, you're going to do anything, okay? So I had a lot of friendships based on people-pleasing and what I would do for them. I'd do this or that, I'd buy them things, or whatever. Well, that had to change, because emotional recovery demands being true to yourself and being honest, concepts that I never looked at before. Concepts like being true and honest and caring about yourself, and not being manipulative or jealous or doing things for the wrong reasons, and checking my motives.

Anxiety Attacks

I didn't get into therapy for probably about two years. My life was so bizarre. I had gotten down to about 220 in my second year in the program and all of a sudden I started having anxiety attacks. I didn't know what they were. All I knew was that I felt funny and felt like I was going to have a heart attack. I remember being at work, and I thought I was having a heart attack and they took me to the hospital.

It turned out that I kept having these anxiety attacks and that I needed therapy. I was under too much stress, you know. The transition was too much for me. At that time I thought, "Oh, here I was the star in OA—two years of abstinence and lose all this weight." I thought, "I work a perfect program. I dodn't need therapy. God's enough for me. God did this, that nobody could do for me. What's therapy going to do?" But I went to therapy, and at the same time my medical doctor tried to medicate me, and I said no. I got really angry, because my doctor said, "Let's put you on medication three times a day."

I knew that any mood-altering substance was bad for me. I had given up the alcohol my first year in the program because I didn't want the extra calories, that's how I looked at it. So I took alcohol back for about three months my second year in the program and realized that I had a drinking problem. Not like a gutter alcoholic, but I knew well enough that I wanted it too much and that alcohol had to go. So I abstained from alcohol and I knew at that point that chemical dependency and mood-altering or mind-altering things were going to be a problem for me, and that meant certain medications, too. So I got really upset because the doctor was saying, "This will really help you." I was on the medication for a month, and I said, "I can't do this. It doesn't feel good to me," to be medicated like that. My therapist was kind of flexible. We talked about it. Unfortunately, he's not an authority on eating disorders or alcoholism. But at that time it didn't matter to me, initially it didn't matter to me.

Then they put me on another drug. It stops your heart from palpitating within twenty seconds. So the symptoms of the anxiety start to dissipate. Well, if you're not learning how to dissipate your own anxiety without using this crtuch, you're going to get dependent on taking things to dissipate the anxiety. And I was filled with anxiety. I was bottled up with some things. The program works in such a way, if you're abstinent, that it gives you what you can deal with when you're ready for it. I knew that, and I was ready to deal with the anxiety at the time that the anxiety was coming up for me. I realized that the first year of the program. I kept things very simple. I just stuck to my food plan and went to meetings. I made a few phone calls, and that was all I could do. That was it. My sponsor said, "Don't do any more. Don't try to do it all this year. This is a lifetime thing."

Depression

So about the second year, when I was having anxiety, I realized there is some more emotional stuff that I hadn't gotten to. I got off the medication, and then, six months into therapy, I was still feeling stoned all the time. I didn't have anxiety attacks as much, but I got this feeling like everything was surreal. I would go out of my house, and I'd feel like crying. I felt like going back to bed all the time, because everything looked surreal to me. I felt like I was in a Dali painting. It was a cold, stark feeling, and I started thinking, "Oh, this life, you know. It's so heavy and it's so cold." I was in a clinical depression, and I didn't know it. I didn't go through treatment, because there wasn't treatment for eating disorders then. There weren't really any doctors at that time that I knew of who understood addiction to food as they do with alcohol.

But they diagnosed me as being in clinical depression, and they put me on an antidepressant. Man, I fought that. The only thing that saved me was, I had a good friend who works in substance abuse, and I checked it out with her. She said many times in treatment they put people on antidepressants, and they're not mood-altering, and that I could trust that if I'm doing the therapy and I'm staying abstinent, that this was going to work for me. I really trusted that, and so I went on the antidepressant, and that was about two and a half years ago.

I'm just coming off it now. I've got about a month more. I went up to what they call the therapeutic level. I was up to that for maybe eight months. I haven't had an anxiety attack for two years, or I haven't had that surreal feeling. It didn't leave right away, you know, which made me angry. I wanted instant feeling good. Matter of fact, I thought with abstinence and losing weight that everything was going to be perfect. I didn't know. I felt life was going to be perfect.

I have been in therapy working on most of my issues, and as I dissipated some of the anger and stuff that was in me, the anxiety decreased a lot, to the point where I don't have to be on an antidepressant for the rest of my life, which was a big fear of mine.

Isn't OA Enough?

I think that episode is really important, too, because I went through a lot of conflict. "Am I a bad person because I'm needing medication? Isn't OA enough? And isn't AA enough?" You know, once I got in the program I think there was this part of me that had so much pride, which wasn't good. I thought, "I can do all this now, because I know how to do it," instead of realizing that it's not a package or a perfect thing. There are going to be things that we have to adjust. You know, you just don't say "I'm going to do this without help," because sometimes you need extra help.

The reason therapy works for me now is because I am abstinent, so I can work on issues. I can work on emotions, and even my spiritual life, and see changes and results from action that I take. Whereas when you are eating and binging, you are stuck. I was stuck in any problem I could tell you about. For some reason, abstinence is an action that enables me to take action emotionally, too. For some reason, the two go together. But with the program and the abstinence, for some reason things change and are always changing, where for most of my life I fought that, I fought change. I was petrified of change. I hated things when they ended. I was petrified of things ending, and I would cry, whether it was reading a book or having my grandmother die.

Dealing with Reality

I couldn't stand the end of things, because I didn't know how to cope. No one gave me those tools. No one told me that life means change, and life means death, and life means good days and bad days. My parents worked so hard at living as if "everything's okay." We'd sit down, and my dad would say—and he still says this—he'd say, "Tell me what happened good today." I would want to say, "You know, Dad, I have nothing good to say, and if I can't tell you how lousy my day was, then I don't feel like I'm being real with you, you know?" But I couldn't. And that was my parents, saying, "Tell me only what was good." Their focus was on not feeling the pain of living life. Now, I'm not saying that by being in OA and dealing with reality that it's only pain. What I'm saying is that I never learned the range of emotions. It was either high or low, there was no middle ground, and that's why therapy has been necessary for me.

My therapist is very good for me too. He's very normal. You really can tell that he is normal, and I laugh all the time, and I always say, "Oh, I'd like to be like you some day." I mean, he has no addiction. His thinking is really normal, clear, not crazy. He's calm.

Somebody Up There Was Doing It for Me

What they talk about in the Alcoholics Anonymous *Big Book*—I think it's in the chapter called "How It Works"—they talk about what they call "a psychic change." I know that I've had a psychic change. How I've gotten to that point, well, I don't know exactly. When you go to meetings and you're abstaining, you are looking for answers to whatever it was that made you eat, and it seems like everything in your life made you eat. So you're going to this place, and you're listening to people talk about how they're not eating compulsively, and how they're living life without compulsive eating, and there's a lot of talk about God. Actually they call it a Higher Power, although they call it God more now, which I think isn't so good, because there are many people who don't believe in God. "Higher Power" seems to be more of a generic term.

But I think what happened was, God helped me stay abstinent, because nothing else was working. It's just like they told me. Every morning, if you get out of bed and you ask God for help, and at night you thank Him, I mean really simple stuff, you will get help. Those days it was "God please help me. I'm powerless over food. Please keep me abstinent today." I read a little morning meditation, which probably didn't sink in at all. I'd get up and eat breakfast, and then at night when I'd go to bed, I'd say, "Thank you, God for keeping me abstinent." It was very simple. All of a sudden, one day, I realized that I had been abstinent for a year. I think that really blew my mind. I think I realized that somebody up there was doing it for me.

Letting Go

It's so incredible, because if you would meet people who knew me five years ago, six years ago, they'd tell you I am a completely different person now. My reactions are different. I mean, I'm still nuts. I still have a lot of the fears, and all the anxiety and that stuff, but I'm just really different. I wish I could figure out what it was that enabled me to change. Because people ask me all the time, people who want it so badly say, "How do you get abstinent? How did you do that?" I have to say, "I really don't know. All I know is that I did what the OA group told me, and I believed that if it worked for them, it could work for me."

The *Big Book* of Alcoholics Anonymous talks so much about character defects: pride, jealousy, anger, resentment, self-will run riot. I could relate to these terms, and I could see all this, that it wasn't so much the food as it was me, the way I reacted or the way I thought. And all of a sudden, I knew I had to think of what the problem really is, talk to someone about it, do what they tell you, and just trust; just turn it over and let it go.

That was a real big one, "Let it go," and it took a long time for me to understand what that meant. I'd ask, "What do you mean, let it go? What does letting go mean?" But what happened was, there was a point when some of the problems felt so hard, or thinking about wanting to eat felt so scary that I just said to myself, "Food is not a choice today." I had to talk to myself. They say, "Fake it 'til you make it." "Fake it 'till you make it" is perfect. Or, "Act as if." If you "act as if" long enough, it will happen to you. I heard those kinds of thoughts and I tried to apply them.

The "letting go" actually worked for me, because there was a sense that, all of a sudden, I could "let something go," like, let a thought go. It started with the thought about food. "Okay, so I want to go binge right now, but I'm not going to for the next two hours." It got down to minutes at times—seriously. There were minutes when I'd say, "I've got to eat. I'm gonna eat." This was in the first eight months. I remember making a phone call to my sponsor. I'd say, "I really want to eat. I feel like I'm going to eat." And she'd say "Tell me what you want to eat," and I'd say, "I want to eat this and this and this." She said, "Do you think you can abstain 'til dinner time and eat what you put in your food plan?" and I'd say, "I think I can do that. Okay, I can commit to doing that."

Committing

For some reason, I took such a deep respect for the word "commit" that when I say it, I feel convinced of it almost at once. That was how I quit smoking and quit drinking. I tried cocaine for a while, and I used the same thing on it.

I got to plateaus in the program, and I'd have to change my food plan. When I was 300 pounds, my food plan was more generous than maybe what an average person would eat. An average person would probably gain weight on what my food plan was at 300 pounds. I don't know how my sponsor did it, but she really helped me have a healthy food plan that tapered me down. But every time I got to a plateau, something had to go in my food plan. What would happen is that I would come up against something, and I'd say, "I'm not losing any weight. Something doesn't feel right." So she would say to me, "Well, why don't you think about what that is?" and I would know right away that something had to go out of my food plan. I knew it the moment I would say to her, "I'm not losing weight, I'm feeling funny." She'd say, "Well, losing the weight isn't the program," and I'd say, "But something feels funny. Something feels funny."

It took me three months on an average when I'd come up against a plateau and, you know what, it is so amazing, because it would be an emotional plateau as well as a physical plateau. I would make some kind of breakthrough, whether it be out of my depression or out of whatever I was into, the problem of the week or the problem of the month. And for some reason, I'd come to the point where I'd say, "I'm getting ready to let go of this thing in my food plan. I'm getting ready to let go of it," and I'd talk about it at meetings. I'd say, "I've got this thing in my food plan that makes me feel guilty," and when you feel guilty about eating, something is wrong. If there is something that is making me feel bad about my food plan, that's not good, because it may be a sign that I am using the food like a drug. I remember this happened with crackers. I had crackers in my food plan, and some other foods that I was using like drugs. I had a lot in my food plan that I don't eat right now. I have a list of things that I don't eat. About twenty-five of them are things that I had on my food plan originally that I don't eat today.

What would happen is, I'd come up against the food, and I'd finally say to my sponsor, "Okay, I'm ready and I'll commit to not eating this today in my food plan." The moment I would say that, and really say, "Today is the day I'm committing to not eating that food," it was like starting over again. It would work. I've never had that food since then. That's what blew my mind, why I'm in awe of the spiritual part of it. Because there's something there that I don't know how to put into words. Maybe I will in twenty years, if I'm still abstinent. Maybe I'll have a better understanding of that power that I tapped, or was given to me through other people. It really was given through people telling me it was okay, that it was going to work. I was always so shocked, and, matter of fact, to this day I won't commit to anything, I won't even use the word unless I mean it, because I know if I commit to it, it works, and I don't always want to give up certain foods or activities.

Adolescence at Age Twenty-eight

When I say "commit," it means I have to be honest. It's not always necessarily with substances, but also with men. I'll say to my sponsor, or she'll say, "You know you're getting a little nuts about these guys, or getting involved with so many guys. Yes, it's exciting. You never had that adolescent development." I'm about thirteen right now, emotionally, with men, and very much in need of going through that. It's amazing, because I see it, and I can't necessarily change it. I have to go through it. I don't react to men like a twenty-eight-year-old woman. I'm still kind of in my early adolescence developmentally.

I know there is another way to be, emotionally. When I feel jealous or angry about certain things, I say, "That is so adolescent," but I can't change it yet. What I can say is that "I know as an adult, I won't be affected the same way." So I know that I'm stuck in emotional adolescence, and it's funny because with men, my sponsor will say to me, "You're getting a little compulsive, don't you think? I think you need to slow down," or whatever.

The Quick Fix—An Avoidance of Life

Whether it's a man or new makeup, the compulsions are more subtle now than eating and being 300 pounds. It still comes out, the compulsion, the fix, the quick fix. I think it is really the addictive cycle, and I think that the quick fix feeling is what I used to block my feelings. That is where the disease begins. I realize that I'm up against the entire strength of Madison Avenue. Our economy depends on getting people to respond like that, to the quick fix. And when I look at it, when I look at it in the big picture, it gets me mad, because I realize it's part of a whole society. Just turn on the TV if you want to see how you can be manipulated.

That makes me mad, so it makes it a little easier sometimes to fight against it. I feel like the quick fix is such an avoidance of living life, about what life is really about.

I have a deep respect for that now, for confronting reality, because for a long time I didn't confront. The moment I started confronting it, it caused pain, but it also brought joy and peace at times that I'd never had. Even if I had serenity for only one hour, it's better than living in total chaos and insanity every other hour. I think it started that way. I had ten minutes of serenity and fifty minutes of pain an hour. It's gotten to be more and more. But that "fix," that need not to feel—it is a part of our society, and it's a part of me, and it's a part of living a life separate from what that Higher Power wants, whatever that Higher Power is.

Escape from Egocentricity

In college, I always wondered what life was about. You know how people go through college and you get stimulated by all the knowledge?

Like all the philosophy stuff. I knew something was missing because I was in living hell. I knew there was another way once I really realized that life was about getting out of yourself, as they talk about in the program. There are so many thin women I see who are so focused on beauty, I mean to the point of obsession. With clothes and make-up and everything. Now I love that stuff, I have so much fun with it. But when I see someone so ego-centered—blocked—I really see why I'm a compulsive eater and how I'm like that. Where another lady is so consumed with self and looking good or being bulimic or anorexic, being thin and pretty, I was consumed with food and fat. But it's the same egocentricity.

The moment I was able to put my needs behind me for a minute and give away something, especially like going to meetings and telling my story or talking about the pain, I was starting to get out of that. I go to meetings and I tell them like it is, and a lot of people, the people who aren't abstinent, have a hard time with me because they don't want to hear it. I'll go and say, "You've got to stick with the winners. It's not okay to be binging or eating a candy bar every other day." If you're doing that and you know you have an eating disorder, then you're being dishonest. It's not that you shouldn't be able to have a candy bar or that you're a bad person, it's that you need to be honest. If you have an eating disorder and you know food is causing you physical and psychological or emotional imbalance, then you are not being honest.

Manipulating the Program

People will sit there and say, "Well, I really know now," because they take the Steps, the program, and they manipulate them. They say, "Well, I had a slip last night, or I binged last night, but I know God loves me, and I know I can forgive myself today. I've come a long way because of that."

I have a great respect for that, I've come a long way too. But what I do is, I say, "I was crying my eyes out last night, I felt awful. I knew I could go and eat a cookie. I knew that would have been a quick answer for me, and would have given me that peace of mind that no human could, but I didn't do it, and I'm here to tell you that it was really painful. I would like to tell you that you don't have to eat." Don't tell me it's okay to eat. Some people try to tell you in OA that it's okay. But it is not.

There are many people who don't "get it"—I mean they don't understand the program. And that's really hard, because I don't want to be judgmental. I can't afford to be, and yet at the same time I have to be true to the fact that if you have an eating disorder and if you want to live life in a way that's healthy, you need to be abstinent and go through that pain. And I get mad. I say, "Don't tell me that you ate a cake, because I'm sitting here dying to go and do that same old thing." I'm not eating cake because I want to get well, so don't tell me it's okay. I don't want to hear that it's okay to eat, because boy, that's just the ticket I need to go right back out and hit the streets. And, if I started, I wouldn't stop.

Stick with Winners

I have friends in OA who stick with it and support each other. I only stick with winners. Right now I sponsor about three people, and I don't sponsor people who aren't abstinent. That wasn't always so. It comes and goes. Sometimes I get really judgmental, and I have to fight it. Well, they say in the program you have to give away what you've got. You have to give away to the level that you're at. I don't know how to tell someone to slip and binge and work the program. I don't know how to give information like that. I know how to give information about eating plans and working through the Steps. That I understand, because that's what I've been doing. So, I need to give to someone who wants that.

Now, there are people who I've sponsored who haven't been able to do that, and I've had to let go of them, or they've let go of me, because it's just too much pain. I've worked with one girl who is a bulimic, who binged and vomited for seven or eight months, and I just prayed and prayed and prayed to hang in with her, believing that she'd get it. She's been abstinent from binging and vomiting for probably two years now. So there are times when I'm really able to help and detach from it, but the majority of my friends and the people I sponsor are all abstinent. I don't know if my sponsor is abstinent. I don't question her about it, but I know she has problems, and this is something we talk about a lot at meetings.

Abstinence Is Not Deprivation

I always tell people that following a food plan is not deprivation. The bottom line is that God wants you to be eating healthy food and a good amount to live and survive. Abstinence is not eating compulsively, or addictively, or for a fix. I know my sponsor is anorexic and bulimic. It's funny that I picked an anorexic and bulimic because I'd always think I would pick someone who was like me, who had been obese. But I didn't. I picked someone who is thin. It's really helped me because I can see the whole illness in its many facets.

Laughter and Mourning

My best friend in the program is a really neat person. She's been in the program about six months less than I have, and she weighed about 400 pounds at the start. Right now, she's about 40 pounds heavier than I am, so we follow each other. We're very close. We're totally different in every way you can imagine, and yet there is such a bond. We'll sit and watch TV, and she's really funny; she really blunt. We'll see all these skinny women, and she'll look at me, and she'll say, "Doesn't it make you sick. It's not fair." And then we'll laugh. We talk all the time about being obese. Even if I lose all my weight, my skin is very stretched out. I have a lot of stretch marks, and it's flabby. And though I exercise, it's never going to be like all those skinny women.

Having weighed 320 is like having had a baby a hundred times probably. There's not that kind of beautiful body that we always dreamed of having. And she and I would always talk about that. What we dreamed of, what we never got. We do a lot of mourning together. She and I are acting out our adolescence right now. We go out every Saturday night to go dancing, just to go through that.

We have so much fun. Guys will come up and ask us to dance, and she'll turn around and say, "They think I'm normal," and we'll just laugh, because we're both still stuck in that. Where do we fit in the range of normality? You know, you're not grossly obese. You're not oddball. You're not Skinny Minnie yet, but you kind of learn that middle range. She and I, we laugh. She's the person who brought the most laughter in my life with the program, because she and I have a sense of humor that won't stop, as far as the eating disorders and talking about it. She'll make jokes about the program, and she'll say things like, "Just for the day, just for this minute, I'll be nice to this person. Even thought I hate their guts, I'm really going to try for just this minute." And we'll talk like that all the time. It's fun; it's great.

Looking Back

My friendships are different now. It's hysterical to me that, as a child I literally was always stealing food, manipulating my friends, my closest girlfriends, whom I've known since age three. When I got in the program, I'll never forget my second year, when an old friend came to a meeting with me just to talk to the people there about how grateful she was, that they were there for me, because she just loved me so much. We were very close, and she was completely normal. I hated her, because she was so normal. I couldn't get it. She said she saw such a transition in me. She saw me change so much that she knew that there was a God then, because she saw me change.

She and I laughed about how when I was a child, we'd get food, and I'd say, "Go get your mom and tell her you want something to eat." And so she would, like a nice little girl. She'd enable me to the max. She would go downstairs and say, "Mom, I want something to eat," even though my mother said I wasn't supposed to eat after school. And she would come back and say "Here," and I'd eat mine within one second, because eating-disorder people eat so fast. Then I would say to her, because she'd eat so slowly, "You know, if I open my hand and close my eyes, I bet if I count to three there'll be a magic surprise." Every time she'd give me her food. To this day, we laugh about it, because she now sees how easily manipulated she was, and I did that a lot. I always had friends who let me eat.

A few of the friends I've connected with over the last four years, I've made amends to for some reason, or have gone back and said, "Hey, I was really crazy, and I wasn't the kind of friend I could've been." Even in high school I had some terrible fallings out with people because I was such a live wire and I was so needy and so sick.

They are all just blown away when I ask them. I ask, "Please tell me how I was, because I don't know any more. You know, I really don't have an understanding." They'd all say how I was always trying to get them to get food for me, and that I was always hiding out, hiding out my food.

You know, I went up to the attic once to get some boxes that I had packed away when I was in eighth grade through high school, some stuff I had saved; every box had candy wrappers in it, empty things, and I was thinking, "This is unbelievable." I'd try to hide, but man I had so much.

Sometimes I Still Hurt

When I look back, I see a big difference in my life. I could get so emotional about that. This is something I talked about this week with my therapist. It's so amazing. There was not a day in my life that people wouldn't make fun of me. I had tacks on my chairs in high school. I had people calling me names; throwing food at me in the cafeteria. I mean, you wouldn't believe it, I would come home crying, saying, "I can't bear it." I got into OA, and from that point on to this day, I've never heard a word about my being fat. I still believe that God took care of me. Because it felt as if I got in the program and there was a little bubble around me. No, I didn't hear any more that I was fat. It was amazing, no one called me names anymore. I couldn't figure it out. I still don't understand how that happened.

I used to say, there's not one day that I went through life that people didn't remind me that I was different. And what I say to my therapist is, "Sometimes, I still hurt. When I think back on the pain I endured emotionally from being rejected by so many people and being laughed at, and then seeing today how everyone looks at me and thinks I'm normal, and they treat me like I'm normal, and guys act like I'm attractive, and after living so long with rejection and dreaming of that possibility, it's so incredible to me."

Therapy—Sometimes the Problems Are Too Big

I don't think its always necessary to go into therapy to adjust to the changes. I think the program is designed so that it can help. Some people who have eating disorders don't necessarily have backgrounds of sexual abuse or alcoholism in their family, or drug addiction or mental illness. These people just have the eating disorder, and their lives are a little simpler. One of my sponsees, she's so funny, she says, "Do you think I need therapy? You're in therapy, and I want to be like you." And I'd say, "Not unless you're having some problem, like an anxiety attack, that is disrupting your life, and working the Steps isn't giving you the answers." I believe it says in the *Big Book* of Alcoholics Anonymous that God made doctors and psychiatrists to help us, not to be people that we lean on, but that God has given them gifts that we need to draw upon at times. It's okay if sometimes your problems are too big, that you're not getting what you need, that you can draw upon these people.

But therapy is not necessary for everybody. I've met so many people in AA and OA who don't go through therapy, and there are some who have used therapy for a temporary period of time and it has worked. I think if a person feels really unhappy and uncomfortable that they might need that support.

I Always Felt That My Needs Were Too Big

I definitely needed someone who would be there just for me. I have a hard time taking. Even with my sponsor, I have a hard time taking. I want to be giving all the time. It's much easier for me to give, because if I take you might not like me, because I might need too much. There's always that, especially with food. There's never enough food; there's never going to be enough love. So I always felt like my needs were so big, that if I had to ask my sponsor for too much, she wouldn't sponsor me anymore. I felt like my needs were becoming so big that I really needed to have a therapist. I really see how needy I think I am at times and how frightened I am of my own neediness. My therapist has to let me know that I'm okay. And then the neediness dissipates, and I think that the neediness is like that emptiness inside that I try to fill with food, and self-hate that developed for whatever reason, that void.

Feelings—I Used Food to Escape Them

I talk about feelings. It's one of my biggest things with my friends, especially guys, because guys have two feelings, lust and anger, and those are their two primary feelings. Something that I talk about all the time is that there are about 150 emotions that a human being goes through, and to start and identify them because we are not taught them. With guys I talk a lot about, "Do you always really want to get in bed and have sex? Or do you really want to be held?"

I am trying to get in touch with that feeling inside that people usually act from and need to get drunk over or need to get high over or need to eat over—that longing. There's a longing inside me lots of times that I think was so frightening that I had to eat to cover it up. Because no one said to me, "Yes, it's scary. Yes, you're right, it's scary." You know, life is so scary, but there are ways to cope. I wasn't taught proper coping skills. I just wasn't.

I can't believe that I wasn't able to catch this stuff as a child. I lived in a fairy tale world that was like musicals. My mother was so big on musicals, with all these happy endings—boy meets girl—and there's always the fairy tale ending. I thought that's how life was. You know, I'm really angry, because no one said that wasn't true. They all supported that, and it's really unfair. It makes women feel inadequate when they don't find Prince Charming, or they don't get what they want. We're told that we're supposed to be married and have kids and have a nice life, and it's such a deception. It's such a setup to feel awful. I think drugs, alcohol, and food are definitely ways to cope with those kinds of feelings.

Dad: Compulsive Personality

My relationship with my parents was very bad for a long time. It's so interesting, because this is where I get confused about the physical problem and the emotional problem. My dad is very highly compulsive, almost neurotic, fearful, really driven—a workaholic personality. He would come home every night at five o'clock, and he would just vent his anger all over my mom, my brother, and me. It was always anger. Then he'd go upstairs and get ready for dinner. Then he'd come down, and we'd sit down. I remember everything would be calm by the time dinner was over. I remember that so clearly.

As a child I knew how to manipulate my dad. If I wanted something (and this is how crazy the thinking was), I would ask him right when he came to the door, and he would explode and say, "Absolutely not." He'd go upstairs, do his thing, come down relaxed. He'd come down like a new man, sit down. Then we'd eat, and after dinner he would say, "I rethought what I told you no about, and now you can have it plus double." So I'd not only get what I had asked for, whether it was money for clothes or something I wanted to do, but he also would give me more. Because he felt so guilty, he'd give me even more. I learned that from my dad, and it was a childish behavior, how to manipulate his moods.

My dad is extremely thin. He jogs about five miles a day. At that time I didn't understand compulsion. I just knew that I was fat, my dad was thin, and my dad's whole focus was me. He'd always worked on trying to get me to lose weight, lose weight, lose weight. He even offered at one time to move to a town in Indiana. He's a salesman, he travels, and he said, "I was in this town in Indiana today, and I noticed there are a lot of heavy people there. Maybe you'd be more comfortable if we'd move to this town." I think he meant well, but it was really hard for me to hear that. It felt like, "Oh they're so ashamed of me," you know.

When we sat down at the table for dinner, he'd monitor when stuff would come around to me. When anything would land in front of me, he'd say to my mom, "Would you pass that to me? I want that right now." He really wouldn't want it. He ate like a normal person. He'd come in sometimes from work and take a handful of crackers or something and eat them, or grab a sandwich, and then he'd come down and eat dinner and get up from the table and get something else. But he was thin. I thought he was normal. Now I think that he is so highly compulsive and energetic that he really didn't gain weight. But I almost think that's he's dry drunk in a way, because he has the same driven, self-willed, very egocentric personality. Very ego-centered—everything revolved around him. A lot of alcoholics have that.

Mother: Pretty Normal

My mother really enabled my dad. It's interesting, she's plump, but she is not obese, and she wasn't plump when I was a child. She was pretty normal as a mom. Now that she is in her sixties, she's plump. She enjoys eating sugar.

She loves sugar, but what I didn't understand was that *she could stop*. And this is what my mom and dad would do: they would never have dessert until I left the dinner table. They'd sit and talk and have tea, and I would go upstairs. I remember at times coming downstairs to get something, and I'd hear paper on the table, like cookies or ice cream, and I'd see them try to hide it—because they didn't want me to eat it, and yet they wanted to have it.

I remember my dad always watching me eat and telling me I should eat less, and why couldn't I lose weight, and taking me to diet doctors, and taking me to all different diet programs. I mean I did everything, as far as diet programs go. I remember him just really trying to control my eating, to the point where it was nuts. I look back on it now, and I have a lot of awareness of how I was living for my dad. It was like I was my dad's biggest problem, and I was sort of a focus for him.

My Brother: He Sexually Abused Me

My brother and I, we don't get along at all, because, well, he sexually abused me for about eight years when I was a kid. It started probably when I was in fourth grade. Now I didn't know what any of it was at that time, and it never went into intercourse per se. Now that I understand, it was more like sadomasochism, where he would make me dress in nylon stockings, he'd measure my breasts, and do this real dominant thing. I really believe that it was because my dad was such an authority figure, so angry and dominating. My brother kind of acted it out on me. There were about six years where he would give me food and money if I let him touch me. I sold myself out because food was about the only thing that mattered to me, plus he also threatened to kill me if I ever told anybody, and I really believed him. I wasn't able to stand up to him until I knew that it had really made my life bad. Matter of fact, I gained a lot of weight when that stuff started happening in my house.

When my brother was abusing me, I felt my parents were not taking care of and not protecting me. I remember the first night it happened. It must have been a trauma, because I remember it. I was in my Brownie uniform, I think at that time there's that feeling in kids of wanting to start rebelling from your mom and dad anyway, and that, connecting up with a sibling or something, felt really good. I wanted that feeling of being close that I wasn't getting from my parents. I remember the feeling of him touching my chest and thinking, this doesn't feel right. I knew it even though I didn't know what sex was. I had no idea.

My parents are almost asexual, I swear they don't have any sexuality about them. My dad and my mom would never talk about it. They would never kiss in front of us; there was nothing. Matter of fact, I was in college when I heard that women had orgasms. Before that, I thought only men had orgasms. It took me a long time to understand what all this stuff was that was empty or missing in my family. But when my brother was abusing me, I don't know what I felt about my parents. I felt like they were in a fairy tale, and we just didn't have any connection. I felt it was my brother and I surviving against them.

My Family: Working Through the Resentment

I see my parents now on a weekly basis. You know, the first year of the program, I was like a holy roller. I loved them, and I forgave them. I've gone through a lot of resentment and working that through. Now, if I have a day when I'm working a good program, I am able to detach and not hook into my dad, who still is very sick. I can be detached with love. But if I'm having a bad day, I'll start to react to him, or tell him what I know about him, and he can't cope with it. When I start shouting at him, telling him what I think he's doing, he says, "You're so manipulative. You're so full of it. You don't really care about me. You're only caring about yourself. Don't try and tell me that this is the way it is, because it's not necessarily that way for everybody." He'll just start laughing, and he'll kind of go into a state of denial where he doesn't know what I'm talking about. And I feel like I'm life, and I'm reality, and I'm confronting him, and he is totally in denial. But, I don't even know what of. You know, I don't know what he is in denial of. So when I see him in denial, it sets me off. My antennas go up; I'm real sensitive.

And so, with my dad, man he can set me off within a minute, if I'm not working really hard at detaching, asking God for tremendous strength, because there's a lot of resentment there. I feel like they didn't give me the love and support I needed or deserved. It makes me mad that my parents didn't help me to be okay. You know, I was never okay.

Growing Up, I Got a Double Message

They did a lot of denial to make sure they never heard me, because they were doing everything they could, within their limits. Now my dad's a toy and candy salesman, so that was also a double message, because he had candy in the basement and toys all the time. I could have anything I wanted. The candy was always there, and he never let me have it, so I'd steal all the time. I stole as a child all the time, mainly food.

My mom would supprt my dad, and they'd stick together about restricting my eating. But when my dad went out of town, my mom would make sure we had dessert at dinner and it would be so much fun. When she'd take me out shopping, we'd always go out for a meal, and we'd always have a fancy dessert. She loves eating sugar and desserts, and that was a big thing. My dad would always say when we'd be on vacation, "You know, you don't have to have dessert, but your mother likes desserts, so we're going to make an exception that you can have dessert." My mother would be back and forth on my eating.

Mother: Needed to Be Like a Little Girl

My mother's really incredible, because she is so strong and assertive in some areas. People in the community love her. She volunteers; she's chairman of this, that, and the other thing. She's a giving, strong, very intelligent woman. In her family role, she and my dad are pretty equal as far as wearing the pants goes.

But she has that part of her that emerges around Christmas or holidays or birthdays that is childlike. She'll talk like a little girl. She'll respond like a little girl. She'll become, for minutes sometimes or for an hour, like a little girl. My mom came from a family of compulsive overeaters who were very wealthy, and they had big everythings. My mom and her sisters, every year, would have a table filled with food for the parties. My dad would always say, "Oh, your mother's family, they always know how to have good food and parties. They're big eaters and drinkers."

My mom would try to re-create what she had in her childhood. Both her parents died when my mom was young. Her dad died of cancer when she was eleven, and her mom died when she was seventeen. She was the youngest of six, and she had to grow up at a very young age, very quickly. But the things she talks about a lot are those days of warmth and love and food, and she tries to re-create that at holidays. Every holiday, she'll try to re-create something. That has been both good and bad for me, because I have that part of me that's so emotional, that gets so caught up in the joy of giving and creating this fairy-tale good feeling. It's very painful sometimes, because a lot of the time I had to support her need for fantasy and ignore my own pain.

I Was One of My Dad's Biggest Problems

I felt that they were seeing only certain things, but I was seeing everything. To this day my mom and my dad and my brother are very connected. When we're all together, man, I'm the oddball, because I'm based in reality.

I was one of my dad's biggest problems, because I'd yell back at him, I would disrespect him. He would say to me, "Show your father respect," and I'd say, "If you respect me, I'll respect you." He, in his rare moments, will come through and say, "You are an incredible human being." When I got out of college, I challenged him a lot on certain issues, and he would stop sometimes and look at it, whatever it was, and say, "You may be right." In those rare moments he responded to me. In a rare moment he'll tell me he really believes in me.

Getting My Needs Met

I have to understand that I can't change him. Now, that took a long time, and it doesn't always stay in mind. Sometimes I still try to make him what he isn't. That's something that comes up in therapy. My therapist would say that this is the key to insanity. "Insanity is repeating the same behavior, again and again, and expecting different results." That was the insanity of many things I do. With my father, it was the insanity of expecting that if I had talked to him this way, if I tell him this, if I act this way, he's going to treat me the way I need him to, the way I'm longing for him too—loving, kind, warm. I've come to realize he's never going to change, unless something really profound happens, and I don't know what that would be. But I've learned to accept the fact that he's not going to give me what I think I need; that my needs can be met other places.

That's another thing I'm learning from the program, too, that there are certain ways to get your needs met, and it's not necessarily the way you think, or the way you want. I want a fur coat, and I think that's going to make me happy, but instead I get a less expensive down jacket. It keeps me just as warm. It may not emotionally make me as happy as what I think I should have. But I'm learning to get what I need, not what I want. I have temper tantrums all the time about that kind of stuff. I have the little girl in me that is active, alive, and well, most of the time.

Relationships with Men: The Cycle of Addiction Persists

It's interesting, because the men I get involved with raise the same issues as my dad. They're not like my dad, but what is alike, is that they are emotionally unavailable. Emotionally unavailable men I choose, because my dad was emotionally unavailable. Now, there have been men that I've met that have been available, and they bore me.

It's something that I work on in therapy. Matter of fact, I'm dating a guy right now, one of two men I'm dating. One is completely normal, is emotionally available, can give and love, and he is boring. Yet I'm trying really hard to stick it out, because I know he is well. I'm not saying that there's not any fun there. What I'm saying is, with him I don't get that quick fix. I want that excitement of the rush that I'm used to in the cycle of addiction. The other guy I'm dating is a musician. He's in the fast lane, and he's really exciting; he's not emotionally available. But boy, when he does look at me, when he does kiss me, I know I got him for that one second. I've worked for a whole week to get that second, and there it is, that whole cycle of the craving and the longing and then the fix. And, here is this other guy standing over here and saying, "I love you, and you're terrific. You're a wonderful human being," and I'm feeling, "I don't know what you're talking about."

I Can See Another Way to Be

Therapy can help me at least see what is going on with these relationships and help me if I'm willing to work out of them. That's the same thing with my sponsor. She'll say, "Sounds unhealthy to me," and I'll think, "I don't want to hear that," because I know it is. I can see it, but I can't always stop. It's hard to unhook. Because of the program, this is the part that is really hard. I have to be honest most of the time. I could be honest and say, "I feel shitty, because I'm doing stuff that I wouldn't normally do for this guy, stuff that I know isn't right." It's not normal to spend all my money on him when he's not spending any money on me. I'm doing a lot for him. I'm driving him, I'm doing for him, I'm this, that. I've always been like that with relationships, and I know it's because of that unavailability. It's what I experienced all my life, and in a weird way it's comfortable for me.

I can see another way to be. I say to myself, "I don't want to be stuck in this. I don't," and I get really resentful when I see myself doing it. Or I'll be impatient. I'll be snippy or something. I'll turn on someone. But I'll see them react like a child, like I would have felt, and I'll say, "Oh my God, I'm so sorry. That is totally uncalled for, and it's not you, it's me." I can see myself do it, and I'll be so mad, because sometimes I can't control it. It's like I'm hooked into that kind of pattern, and it's painful because I don't want to be like that. I can see another way to be, and I'm getting there.

Preface to Frannie

J ody, Irene, Dave, and Jennifer present variations of patterns of compulsive eating. Frannie suffers not only from compulsive eating but also from the practice of vomiting or purging. This is commonly called "bulimia," although bulimia is actually the proper term for binge eating. Many bulimics, such as Irene, do not practice vomiting.

Like Dave, Frannie is alcoholic. Her story is somewhat different, though, because Frannie was very good at keeping up appearances. She *looked* normal. She had periods of weight gain and periods of starvation or vomiting when she was very thin, but she was never obese to the degree found in Irene, Dave, or Jennifer, and her thinness was within the acceptable limits for women. Also, people around her saw her eat, so there was no evidence of starvation. To all appearances, Frannie was okay.

But Frannie was not okay. Frannie's eating illness and alcoholism were killing her. The progression of her disease is similar to the pattern already seen in Jody, Irene, Dave, and Jennifer. She presented symptoms of body obsession and compulsive eating patterns in grade school. As she grew up, the diet and weight-gain cycle began. With high school, the normal stress of competition and peer pressure increased, and so did her feelings of inadequacy. Her people-pleasing became acute.

In high school she began purging. "What a great idea," she thought. Purging seemed like the ideal solution to the problem of "How can I eat and not gain weight?" In college, Fran progressed rapidly in her vomiting practices, and lost a great deal of weight.

Even when she was thin, Frannie still felt fat, another common characteristic of an eating illness. However, Fran did feel "more confident and extroverted," so she began to party, go out with boys, drink, and smoke pot. This is another behavior associated with an eating illness—the tendency to be excessive, the inability to balance one's life. In her case, Frannie threw herself into the new party lifestyle and flunked out of school.

At that point she had another experience common to many who have suffered with an eating disorder—ineffective interpretative therapy. When she was reinstated at school, Frannie sought help from the psychologist at the student health center. She was told she wasn't loved enough, and that's why she was purging. Her immediate response to this was outrage: "The one thing I knew I had in my life was that I *was* loved enough by my family." Then she was given a diet that resulted in a temporary weight gain, which invariably will happen when a bulimic stops purging.

This approach to Frannie's problem was guaranteed to fail, and did for two reasons. First, Frannie could not stay with this approach when it made her gain weight. She did not understand that temporary weight gain is the inevitable result once purging stops and healthy eating begins. Frannie was obsessed with her weight, and literally measured her self-esteen by the bathroom scale. A weight gain threw her into a panic. She needed a treatment program that would focus on changing the eating behavior while de-emphasizing weight. Until she could learn to accept her natural body weight, which was greater than her ideal weight, she needed continuous group support to reinforce her behavior changes. And, by her own admission, she needed the spiritual growth fostered by a Twelve Step program.

The second reason was the assumption that merely providing her with a theoretical reason *why* she purged would in itself enable her to stop and stick to the diet. Interpretive therapy is a lengthy process, and it can take many years for a cognitive or perceptual change to translate into a behavioral change. Frannie couldn't wait that long. She needed immediate intervention to deal with her eating disorder.

Frannie was lucky. Her family intervened. Unable to help herself, completely isolated, she might have died from the complications of her cross-addiction—alcoholism and bulimia. The degree to which her thinking was impaired is evident in the intervention scene. The fact that she can now recognize it is a tribute to her successful recovery.

Another important characteristic of Frannie's illness is that her purging had become an obsession by itself. The need to vomit was as acute as the compulsive need to eat was to Irene or Jennifer. They are variations of the same disease. Frannie subscribes to the disease concept of addiction, and credits her recovery to the treatment program's emphasis on directly addressing the eating and purging behavior within a context of group support and spiritual growth.

In summary, Frannie's story brings together the elements of the disease and recovery already seen in previous stories, with the additional complication of purging as a form of the compulsion. Her story also offers an example of intervention to initiate treatment, a method that may not always work but may, as in Frannie's case, save a life.

FRANNIE

Body Obsession in Grade School

I remember when I was in fourth grade taking ballet lessons. I was a normal-sized kid at the time, but I remember quitting ballet because I thought my thighs were too big. Swimming in the summer time was a problem. I would get out of the pool and wrap the towel around me right away. Now I look back and I can see that I was very normal in size. I did not have a real problem with huge thighs or swimsuits. But I had hidden eating patterns. In third grade, I would make these bizarre concoctions of grotesque food, all sugar and white flour, and hide and eat them. When I was in fifth grade I started to gain more weight. All along, my parents and the doctor had been saying, "Well, it's just going to take Frannie a while to lose her baby fat." But I didn't, and when I got into seventh grade I went to my first diet club.

Dieting and Gaining

My mom has always been on a diet; never grotesquely overweight, but always weight conscious. So we went to a diet club together. I was always successful at diets, but I always returned to the old eating habits. My dad could eat half his pie and push away the rest, and only eat until he was full, but I did not have that capability. Every time I went on a diet, I lost weight fast, was very strict with myself, never cheated, and was very serious. But I'd reach goal weight and blow it. I have a weird metabolism. I remember once in high school, I went on a liquid diet and lost a lot of weight. I was very successful at it, and went off the diet, and that day drank a glass of orange juice and gained two pounds!

I started to weigh more as I got into sixth, seventh, and eighth grades. In eighth grade, I remember being in camp and afraid someone would see my physical, because my weight was high. I can't remember what it was, but I know my weight was high. But it didn't keep me from anything. I was good in sports; swam, did archery, all that kind of stuff.

Shopping for Clothes Was Horrible

I remember eighth-grade graduation was traumatic because I could not find any clothes that fit me. Shopping was always horrible. Clothes I liked would never fit. I was wearing large-size clothes, 12 to 14, and in eighth grade that's not normal. All my friends were skinny little cheerleaders.

I remember the trauma of buying an eighth-grade graduation dress. It was just horrible. My mom and I went to tons of stores and finally found something that was just "ugh." But it was the only thing that I could fit into that went with the school code of what you had to wear: colors, length, and all that stuff for graduation. To this day, I still hate shopping, because shopping was a pain in the neck for a really long time. I would cry every time. My mom and I would be there, and I'd be crying because I couldn't fit into the clothes.

My sister, who is five years older, was always thin, and could eat anything she wanted. Well, everybody in my family could do it, except for my mom. My mom was always on diets, and we know now that diets don't work. They make you gain weight. What a cruel joke. But I was the fat one, and everybody else was skinny. My younger sister could eat anything. We would be on family vacations, and I'd be eating my half a grapefuit for breakfast, getting fat, and she would be eating French toast with butter.

High School Traumas

When I got into high school, I don't remember being overly overweight in freshman or sophomore year. But I think I was just continually inching up, inching up, inching up in weight and not really being aware of how high I was going.

My junior year, there were a couple of traumatic things that happened. I remember my brother came in, and I'd bought some new blue jeans. My brother saw them, and said, "Who has this size blue jeans?" He thought they were my dad's, and they were mine. Another time, I was in a play, and in the part I had, two guys had to lift me up. I was playing a ghost, an apparition in a dream, and they had to pick me up. One guy, I met in the hallway afterwards. I remember I was carrying some mugs I was selling for the pep club, and the guy said to me, "You really ought to lose some weight." Really tacky and really blunt. I remember I was really angry. I had those mugs in my hand—I really did want to bash him with them. That wasn't a normal, reasonable reaction. After that I lost a lot of weight.

Introduction to Purging

In my junior year, my brother was dating a cheerleader. I remember him telling me about them going out to dinner, and she would do this strange thing—she'd go and vomit after eating. I had never heard of it, but it was not disgusting to me, and I thought, "What a great idea." Soon after that, I started to do it. I was seventeen years old when I started to vomit. I was very "progressed" in my vomiting capabilities, for lack of a better word, when I started. I was very good at it. I also was very obsessed with the whole idea of losing weight. What a great idea—I can eat and not gain weight. So I had a license to kill, you know. Here is this great trick you can use, and almost immediately I exhibited starving and binge eating and purging habits. The second time I ever did it, I had been on a diet. By this time, I'm off regular diets, and I'm doing obscure, bizarre diets. You know, saltines and grapes for a week. Five saltines and ten grapes all day, very insane, and then, of course, going out and eating ice cream and potato chips and just junk. The second time I ever purged, I had been on this starvation kick, and I ate a carton of yogurt. Now yogurt is not fattening. It is if you eat ten, but one carton of yogurt is not going to kill me. But I really felt, "I'm too full, I don't like this," and that was the second time I vomited. The first time I had really eaten too much, and thought, "Why don't I try this?" But here I was, only the second time, a long way progressed into starvation.

I Had Friends but Never Felt Popular

Then I just sort of went along, and my senior year I really didn't vomit very much, but continued to gain weight, gain weight, gain weight. After my senior year, I went out west with some friends from high school. We just played around and goofed around, and drove in the mountains, and hiked, and drank, and ate. By the time I went to college, my freshman year, I weighed 180. I had probably always stuck around 150 to 160 in high school.

When I got to college, it was as if I had an opportunity to be a different person than I always was in high school—shy, introverted, blimpy. In high school I was always in various different cliques. I knew friends in the cool clique, I knew friends in the druggy clique, I knew friends in my clique, and girl's club, and pep club, and from various suburbs, people who had been at my high school, but I never felt popular. I think I did have a group of about five to ten girls that I was really close with. Probably a couple of them knew how I felt about my weight. I know my best friend did, because we felt exactly the same, like blimpy wallflowers. We were not really blimpy, you know. If you looked at me, or you looked at my senior picture or my pictures throughout high school, you would not say, "That kid looks obese." But I felt that way.

I Didn't Run Around with Boys

When I went to college, I wanted to change. It's because I never dated. I never talked to guys in high school. My brother was in a band, and the only guys I ever talked to in high school were these two guys that were from my town and then the guys in my brother's band. I never felt popular, partly because I didn't run around with boys. The high school I went to was very competitive. Everybody was pretty and skinny, and I was just rather average. When I started my junior and senior year all the friends I hung around with were like me, just sort of average. But suddenly they had boyfriends, or they were in honors classes, and I was just sort of floating around. I don't remember being jealous. I just remember knowing that I couldn't have dated. I don't think I knew how to relate to guys. I was so shy and so introverted that if one looked at me, I didn't know how to handle it. So I ran around with groups of girls.

It's sad when I think back on it. I became like the chauffeur for everybody. I was an intense people pleaser. They had address parties when I was in high school, so if there was a party at 123 Main Street, we would buy some beer, or whatever, and I'd be driving the car, and they'd go in the party, and I'd sit in the car alone and listen to the radio and drink a beer or two until they would come back. I would never go into one of these big, huge parties. I felt too uncomfortable. It was sort of sad. I just hung around and drove them all over.

Purging Escalates in College

I went to college a thousand miles away. Only one or two people from my high school went to this college, so I decided I would change. I started purging more. I would eat minimal diet food and then purge. I would have a salad for dinner and then purge. To make myself feel full, I would have a cup of hot cocoa or something. Then, on the weekends, I would go out and eat more. We would go out for pizza, or submarine sandwiches. From the beginning, there was always someone who I was friends with who was aware of my eating disorder, who was aware of the fact that I purged. When I came home for Christmas vacation, I had lost 30 pounds my freshman year, first semester. Nobody goes to college and loses weight. I was the exception, and I heard, "Oh gosh, Frannie, how did you do it?" I was so proud, and I lost 20 more pounds second semester. I lost 50 pounds in a short period of time, in a really unhealthy way. I was down to 130 or something. I looked a million times better, but I still felt fat, and no matter how thin I got, I always felt fat. I'm 5 feet, 8 inches, and in my sophomore year I got down to 117, but I still felt fat. I know now I must have looked sick, just bony. Because 5 foot 8 and medium size at 115 to 117 is really pushing it. But I did feel fat, *always* did. But I also felt a little more confident and extroverted being thin.

Failing in School

I did horribly in school, and that had never happened before. In high school I was a goody-two-shoes. Basically, I was Suzy High School, and this wasn't the case when I got to college. I flunked out my freshman year.

This totally blew me away. I had to reapply to get back in the next semester. I wrote that I had failed because I had lost weight and that I now was dealing with guys and that I never had a social aspect to my life before. It still bothers me that I'm not done with college. I have two semesters left. It bothers me because I come from a nice suburb, and I think ninety-nine percent of my high school went to college, and everybody finished, and everybody's successful, or married, with adorable kids and a rich husband. I don't fit into any of those categories.

Ineffective Counseling

By sophomore year, I was beginning to party more. I never did hard drugs in high school, but I now began to smoke pot. My best friend and I would occasionally smoke pot in high school, but rarely. I drank some in high school, but when I got in college, I began to drink more and party more. I remember my sophomore year, I began to realize that my eating habits were wrong. I didn't know that there was a word "bulimia"; I didn't know I had an eating disorder. I just knew that I wanted not to purge and not to gain weight.

I went to the student health center at my college. I told them about my purging. I had a best friend at the time who knew about this, and we would eat together and go purge. Turn the water on, and go purge. I told them all about it at the student health center, and they told me that I had not been loved enough; that's why I exhibited this behavior. Here's a diet, and you should be fine. They made me talk with a psychologist, I think twice, and I hated it. It was really uncomfortable. I come from a totally loving family, and I was furious that they had told me I was not loved enough. The one thing I knew I had in my life was that I was loved enough from my family! Then I went on their diet, and I gained weight! Now I understand that if you have been purging, when you eat you are going to gain weight. At the time I had no clue, and I gained weight, a couple pounds, very fast, and I thought "this isn't working," so I stopped. So that was all I tried.

My "Dumb Habit"

I was just sort of piddling along in school and continuing to eat more. Now I was progressing in the disease. I guess that's the only way to put it, because initially I used vomiting as a way to eat and not gain weight. Then I used it as a way to lose weight. Now I was just *using* it. It was just something I did, and I used to call it my "dumb habit." That's how I referred to vomiting. People knew; I did not keep it a secret. If I could, I would keep it a secret, but if people found out, they found out. That's the way it went. My junior year I continued to do the same thing, and it was bad. That year, I had a bizarre thing happen to me. I don't know if it was a seizure or a dizzy spell. I really don't know. I remember I had eaten a pizza and purged, and then was drinking some beer. I got up off the sofa and went into my bedroom to take my clothes off, and walked into the door. Then I walked into the bathroom and bashed around. I had not had what I thought was a lot to drink, so I really think it was the combination of eating a ton of food, then no food, and then drinking. My roommate came in, and I was down on the floor. She helped me into bed. I think I was beginning to get into really poor health. I really have had no permanent consequences of my bulimia. I've always had crummy teeth. So that is not anything new to me. The only thing that I had was the teeth marks on my hand from sticking my finger down my throat.

Living Abroad—Gaining Again

In my junior year, my weight stayed around 130. It was always hard for me to maintain that. I always strived for it, but it was hard for me to maintain. I was a language major, and the next year I went to school in Europe. I went to school, and I lived with a nice old lady, and we got along very well. The problem was, in Europe, in the bathrooms, there is a toilet, but no sink with running water. It was hard for me to purge, because I always used to turn the water on. In my junior year in college I would do a lot of hand laundry, would take a lot of showers not to let my roommates know what I was doing in the bathroom. This year was very hard because there was no running water available where the toilet was. But I continued, and the lady was old, and I was quiet, fast, and real good at it. And I would sneak out a lot. I've done this from day one. You know, sneak eating—going and buying food, pretending it's for a bunch of people, and then eating it all. I gained a lot of weight. I know I got up to 150. It was horrible. I looked horrible. I was fat, blimpy, and gross. But did great in school.

That summer I traveled and, of course, again went on a very crash, icky diet. I carried this heavy backpack, drank soda and ate carrots and ice cream, and I lost weight. If the opportunity presented itself, and I could purge, I would. Then I went back to the States, took a year off, and just hung around. I don't really remember much about that year. I traveled around and visited people I knew. I just bummed around, didn't work or anything like that, but I visited friends and relatives.

Back Home—Coming Apart

At the time, I said that I needed to drop out, because it was a very huge culture shock. It is hard to come back to school, but I now look back and realize that I should have gone right back, or only taken a semester off. When I finally went back to college, it was not a very good year. I dropped out of my classes. I hibernated. Prior to this, I had always lived with people, and this was the first year that I lived by myself. I didn't have to hide anything, so I'd eat. I didn't go to class. I'd unplug the phone, didn't answer the door. That year really is a fog. That year was as bad a bottom as I had later, right before I went into treatment.

It was horrible. Before I learned the trick of unplugging the phone, my older sister called me up, and I was angry. Who the hell was letting the phone ring twenty times, fifty times? I picked up the phone, and I yelled, "I don't want to talk!" I was very angry.

Now I had begun to drink more. I drank a lot of beer or wine. I didn't drink hard liquor, not that there is a difference. I came back home, and now when I think about it, I was really sick at the time. My mom now tells me that they got me home on some false pretense. I have no idea; I don't remember that. I found an old bag of letters, bank statements, and things like that from that last year. There were a million bounced checks. All the letters that my mom, my dad, and my younger sister would write me were, "We love you, Frannie. You're okay. It will get better," that type of thing. When I recently reread them, it was very sad, because I had no clue. I don't remember getting those letters. I don't remember very much of that year.

Physical Decline

When I came back home, probably the biggest mistake I ever made was moving into the city. I lived at home for a while and worked downtown at a bank. I had a seizure that year. I was doing cocaine at the time, had been drinking, and, of course, no food. I don't know what caused it.

I was living with my parents, but they were not home that day. My younger sister happened to be home, and I remember sitting in the kitchen. I was writing a check. This is not very funny when I think about it. I looked at the check, and it was not my handwriting. That's what I said to her. I said, "This is not my handwriting. This just looks real weird," and I knew I needed to eat something. So, instead of getting what a normal person would eat, bread and butter and jam or something good for them, I stood up to get five peanuts. If I ate and I knew I couldn't purge, I would eat minute amounts of food, like five peanuts, or one cracker. That's what I stood up to get, and I had the seizure. I don't remember anything until I came to, and the paramedics and the cops were in my living room, and my younger sister was in there freaking out. It was very scary for her.

Even after this happened, my parents still didn't know about my eating disorder. They were sort of avoiding it. It was easier not to pay attention, I think. Everyone knows young women in high school and college have very erratic eating habits, and it is common for someone to starve for days. I don't know if they knew at the time, but they never discussed it. After the seizure incident, I carried on as normal. I was very good at keeping up appearances.

Purging in the Hospital

This happened right before Christmas, and I got out two days before Christmas. I was there for four days, and I was still purging when I was in the hospital. They questioned me about drugs, and I do believe I lied. I don't believe I told them I'd been doing coke and drinking the night before. They did a spinal tap and an EEG, and put me on Dilantin, just in case. They just said it was a freak thing, and I had a seizure just once. I didn't have epilepsy or anything.

If they had asked me about food or purging, I probably would have told them. A lot of people in my life knew. I'm not like the normal person who came into treatment and it was the first time that they ever told anybody. It was not my big secret. I didn't feel really intense shame about it unless people found out under the wrong circumstances. I remember one time, when I was a sophomore in college, I was friends with these two girls, and one of the girls was the girl I would binge and purge with. This girl and I once went over to an apartment right near campus, right near my dorm. I walked in, and there was a bunch of guys there, and my other friend introduced me as, "This is the girl I told you about who vomits." Another time, one of my friends who was a really good friend of mine, the first guy I had ever really met and known as a friend, told me, "Well, I know how you lost all that weight." It really was humiliating.

After I got out of the hospital, I wasn't supposed to drink. I had to be driven everywhere because I wasn't allowed to drive. That was horrible, because I worked and took the train downtown, and my mom had to drive me to the train in the morning and pick me up after work. On Fridays, we'd all go out for drinks after work, and I'd have to catch the 6:31 train back up to mom and dad's house. I wasn't supposed to drink but I did. My friend the nurse said, "You know you did everything wrong." Obviously, to continue to purge in the hospital shows how distorted I was in my thinking.

Maybe One Meal a Month

At this point, I was not capable of keeping anything in my stomach. I had an intense fear of gaining weight, and even one meal was just horrendous for me. I would be full for days. I never ate one meal at home with my family that I ever kept down. This is one of the things that I do consider a miracle today, that I am alive, because I bet I didn't eat a meal for years. I got probably a cumulative amount of one meal a month, and had done this for ten years or so. It's amazing that I am not deformed, that I am not physically or mentally incapacitated.

I would eat with my family, then I'd always go purge. But I was good at keeping up appearances. I was really good at showing I was okay. My mom would pick me up, and I'd stop off at the hamburger joint in town, and I'd buy two of everything. My mom would only see one, so I'd go into the library or family room, and snarf down one, and then go purge. I'd do that kind of stuff a lot.

When I Couldn't Purge, I Couldn't Eat

That year, in May, we went on a family vacation, and we camped the whole time with a group of people. There were no toilets. It was the first time I had ever not purged. There was sumptuous food on this trip, and everybody else gained a ton of weight. But I lost about 10 to 15 pounds in ten days. I did not eat. I never ate breakfast. I would have a little bit of food in the palm of my hand for my lunch—some lettuce, tomato, avocado, and mayonnaise—and eat a piece of cheese. That was my lunch. Dinner I'd play with, and make it look like I ate, because I knew I couldn't purge, and therefore couldn't eat.

I lost a ton of weight. It's funny, I look back at the pictures now from when I was thin, and I can see I felt confident. That's all there is to it. You could even tell by looking at the pictures that I felt confident. The way I was standing, the way I'm holding my body—I felt confident.

This one girl on the trip came up to me who was very overweight, visibly overweight, and asked me if I was anorexic. I remember laughing inside because I knew I was bulimic. By then I knew I was "bulimic," but I didn't really understand it. I read all sorts of things on anorexia and bulimia and even wrote to places for help, and still never had a clue. It was like, "I have brown hair and I'm bulimic." Nothing. So I remember laughing at that, and then I remember overhearing two different conversations in which people said, "This girl is anorexic." By then I was back to 115 pounds, and my family tells me that it was very scary to look at me. I was just a mouth and a neck. But my family never *said* anything to me, although my younger sister tells me they were always glad when I started to gain weight. I was always really angry that I was gaining weight, but everybody else was always glad, because I looked sickly.

Incapable of Everything

After that year, I moved into the city. I lived at a great address, the whole party neighborhood. Now I look back on it and say, "How perfect." Here I was, this very sick person, no friends, contact with my family was my only life, my only support system, and I moved down to the city to this great address. I'm not a success. I'm not out of college. I don't have a job, but I must be okay, because look where I live. I had this humongous facade. Went back to college, did great, got A's in my classes, met a friend, started to date when I moved downtown. For a while everything was okay. I was partying. I was meeting people. Then, of course, it took over again. My eating disorder made it impossible for me to go to school, to have friends, to be comfortable at parties, to answer the phone, to do anything. I could not. I just was really incapable of everything.

Obsession Intensifies—Drinking Gets Worse

I was obsessive about my appearance, about food and purging. I always thought that I couldn't eat breakfast because it would start me off for the whole day. That's not true, because I eat breakfast every day now, and it doesn't start me off. But back then I would not eat breakfast. I would drink some tea on the way to school, and then I'd eat something like an apple and some sunflower seeds for lunch. Then I would come home, and I'd either stop at some fast-food type of place, or else I'd stop at the grocery store and pick up food, and then would proceed to eat all night.

When I was living in town, that's when my drinking began to get worse. The only way that I knew to stop eating and purging was to drink, because I would not purge alcohol. It would be the same kind of thing if I was in a social eating situation. I would drink because it totally cut my appetite.

Those last few years in town are all sort of jumbled together. I was not working. I was getting older. I was feeling frustrated, thinking I'm never going to get married. I was living on my income from dividends and stuff, and not doing anything with my life. Now my mom says, "Oh gosh, did we enable you," and I say, "You enabled me not to have to steal."

My Whole Life Was Food

At the very end I was eating a lot of food a day. Any waking moment was either spent on making grocery lists, grocery shopping, coupon cutting, recipe looking, copying recipes from newspapers, eating, purging. I mean my whole life was food. I lost all contact with friends. I didn't pay my phone bills, and my phone would be disconnected. If I did have the phone hooked up, I wouldn't answer. Finally, one year, I got an answering machine for Christmas, because everybody knew I didn't answer the phone. They got me an answering machine, because I was terrified of answering the phone. I wouldn't open my mail. It was hard for me, at the end, to even go down to get my mail. I lived on the third floor, and if I didn't have to go out for food, I didn't go down to the mailbox. I never opened my mail, just looked at it, shoved it in the corner.

My sister got married that June, and I think now it probably was traumatic for me. She's four years younger and was getting married and I'm older and wasn't getting married. At the time, people would say to me, "Well, ya' know, our youngest got married before our oldest," and I'd be so angry at these ladies who talked to me this way. Because, actually, I felt no animosity toward my sister. I was happy for her. She had been dating this guy for seven years. But probably, I bet, inside I was sad. I remember one time, and this really bothers me, I came to address wedding invitations and I was drunk. So it must have bothered me.

Needing Help—Unable to Follow Through

By then I was doing things like that, sending huge messages all over the place. I wanted one day just to appear at my parents' doorstep and say, "I don't do it anymore." But I didn't know how to stop it, and I didn't want to ask for help. I thought one of my greatest traits, my main characteristic, was that I was an independent young woman, so I didn't want to ask for help.

But I did ask my brother-in-law for help, and he kept it a secret. He didn't tell anybody. He investigated for me, found this place downtown, right down near my apartment. I went there, and they were very helpful. It was on an outpatient basis, which I now know to be ridiculous, because here I was binge eating and purging probably ten times a day, and how could I do outpatient once or twice a week? I went twice, and then I had to show this economic background, or whatever, and I couldn't do that. I would have to ask my dad for tax information, so I couldn't do it. I couldn't let my parents find out.

By now my family doctor also knew about this and about my drinking. I would always lie about how much I drank and how much I smoked, and I remember when I was in the doctor's office, I had to hide my hand, because I had those teeth marks. He gave me names of psychiatrists who dealt with eating disorders. I don't recall if that's what he called it. I don't know, because I had never heard the words "eating disorder" until I got into treatment. But again I could not take action. I continually asked for help, in weird ways, but I could not follow through. And would become very angry when someone asked me if I'd followed through.

I Knew My Life Was Horrible, but Didn't Know Why

I was doing weird things. I'd come up to my parents house for dinner on Saturday night, and I'd stay for two weeks. My electricity was cut off a couple of times. My phone was disconnected. We would talk about it. Their response was, "Poor Frannie. What's going on with Frannie?" But never any connection to eating behavior. My mom always looked for the best, and I did the same thing. I'd whitewash everything.

I remember driving up to my parents' house from my apartment and always drinking one or two beers. I couldn't even go to my parents house without drinking.

I felt I was seventeen. I found out in treatment that you feel like the age you were when you started being active in your disease. That's when I started purging, when I was seventeen. So I felt like this insecure, unsuccessful, little twerp, whatever, when I went up to my mom and dad's. My brother has told me that when I'd leave, my mom would say, "Oh, she is doing so much better." He'd be angry, because he could see right through it. He'd say, "No, Mom, Fran is not okay." He told me he was the ogre, but everybody else kept insisting, "Fran's okay. Fran's okay, Fran's okay," and he would be saying, "Really, look at it. She's not."

I would never have gone into treatment on my own. I had no clue about my eating disorder. I had never heard of OA. I *never* thought I was a compulsive overeater. I had no clue that I had trouble with alcohol, that I was an alcoholic. I knew my life was horrible, but I could not have told you why. I had no clue as to why my life was horrible, because I knew I was capable. I could go to college and get straight A's. I could hold a job and do a good job. But I had no clue as to what was wrong with my life. By this point, my younger sister and my older brother really weren't even talking to me or socializing with me. I would be saying the same thing over and over, "My life is lousy," but I couldn't do anything about it. I would just sit there and complain.

I had begun to drink too much. My younger sister was very uncomfortable with that. One time I burned the phone book. I left a cigarette on it and burned it, so she left it open so the burn would show. She did things like that. Her husband had a stepfather who had gone through alcoholism treatment, so my brother-in-law knew about Al-Anon. He knew how to respond. And finally they did an intervention.

Eating, Drinking, and Isolation

By then I was not answering my phone at all. I was beginning to eat all day long, and I was not even going out of the house. I remember, Mom got sick, she had pneumonia after my sister got married, and I stayed there and took care of her. Then I decided to go home, and I never left my house after that.

I really had just a heavy duty month and a half at the bottom. I guess I was ready for the intervention. My mom wrote me a letter saying, why don't you come up for dinner on such and such night? I received the letter the next day. I was not answering the phone now. Here I lived twenty miles away from them and they were writing me letters. Then they wrote me a letter the next day saying, "We can't do it this night. How about the next night?"

So that day, the day I was supposed to go to dinner, I remember I sat in my apartment. I had gone to the store that day and stocked up. This was not unusual; I would spend $30, $40 a time in the grocery store. I was going probably every other day, spending a lot of money on food, and eating all day long. My capacity to hold food in was down to nothing. I didn't eat a lot of junk. I ate meals, mainly omelets and toast and sausage. I could only eat half and would stick it in the oven, go purge, then come back and finish. I figure I was purging anywhere from ten to fifteen times a day, on average. Because I ate at least four times a day, and I purged at least two times each time. That's at least eight to ten times a day.

At night, I'd start drinking, because that stopped me from eating. My schedule was so goofed up. I'd start drinking at eleven o'clock watching TV, and I'd drink throughout the night. I'd stay up and watch stupid TV, and just "veg" in front of the television. I'd go to bed when the morning news shows came on, sleep all day, get up with the evening news, the national news, and then eat, and then drink. It was just this vicious thing. By now, I'm paranoid, and thinking that people can see me from across the hall, from highrises across the way. I never opened the blinds. It's spooky to think about.

The day of the dinner, I remember, I sat there all day, and I thought, "Wow, I really don't want to go up there for dinner." Normally, perfect me would have called them and made up some excuse. This time I didn't, and it just got closer and closer. I had it timed to the minute to how late I could eat, then purge, take a shower, and get out. I just remember watching the clock. It was like I didn't care.

They Did an Intervention

That night (I have talked about this to my mom), they had a suitcase packed for me, which she said was horrible. She said it was as if she was packing the clothes for the morgue, and that I was dead. Later I found out that they had been in touch with a couple of treatment places. They went to a hospital where my mom is involved. She was there with my younger sister checking out the eating disorder unit and saw a bunch of people she knew in the hallway and decided against putting me there. Then they called up another hospital, and the lady was very helpful there. She said, "This is not normal for me to refer you to somewhere else, but we only deal with eating disorders, and it sounds like your daughter is an alcoholic as well." By now I had started to pass out on the sofa at their house, so it was apparent. Also, I never threw out bottles. I put them in this one dresser in my bedroom. I know that was just me screaming for help, because why wouldn't I throw them away? Anyway, they opened the dresser one time, and I had a whole row of bottles lined up—wine, beer, scotch (by now I was drinking scotch)—and they had to see it. So the lady at the hospital said, "I tell you what, check out this other place, they deal with cross-addictions. Because I do know if you don't deal with both at the same time, one will come back, and she'll go back out there." The lady said to my mom, "This girl is terribly progressed. She is dying. She should have been here last week." Freaked the hell out of my parents.

My mom talks about how they didn't know how to do the intervention. They had known about my problem for a while now, because apparently I'd get up from the table, and I always thought I was being so smart, pretending I was going to do the dishes and things like that, but actually I was purging. Everybody would look at each other and think, "Oh, God, there she goes again."

I Wouldn't Let Them In

That day, time went by, and I was sitting there in the middle of a binge. Oh, it was horrible. The buzzer was downstairs, and I knew it was my parents. Now, mind you, my apartment is trashed. I haven't been out in weeks. I'm a mess. I look just horrible, zero care about personal appearance or apartment. That was something I had always been very meticulous about before, my apartment and my appearance. So I didn't let them in.

My mom, dad, my younger sister, and her new husband—they had been married for two months—were at the door. I know it's them, and now I'm angry. It's like, "Who the hell are you, for you to come and invade my privacy?" That's how I always felt every time I got a letter, every time I got a phone call. Sometimes they sent me telegrams. It would be like, "Get out of my face. You're invading my privacy." I didn't let them in, and they were down there, doing da-da-da-da-da-da-da with the buzzer, so I would know it was them. It's nine o'clock on a Saturday night, and I didn't let them in. All of a sudden, somehow I know that they are going to be able to get in, so I'm frantic. I'm running around the apartment. I'm sort of cleaning things, put on different clothes, trying to make things look relatively normal, which is a joke, because the apartment was trashed. Next thing I know is, right in my hallway, right in front of my door (if someone walked by you could hear the floor creak), I hear the floor creak. Knock, knock at my door. I yelled, "What!" really loud. It really made me mad. They sent my younger sister because she and I were very close, and they knew I would open the door for her. That's why she was brought along. They knew I wouldn't open the door for them, but they knew I'd open the door for her. Then she said— Punkin was my nickname—she said, "Punkin, it's me," so I finally decided to let her in. I thought only she was there, but I opened the door and they were all there. I was really angry, and I swore at them, incredible vehemence, I mean just pure hatred. And I was in the middle of a binge on top of it.

Anger and Resistance

I can talk about it now and I don't cry, because they did save my life, but at the time I was so angry at them, I just couldn't believe it. They were saying, "We're taking you now." They had the suitcase packed, and they were ready to take me to treatment. They were talking about how it can be treated medically, and I was saying, "What the hell are you talking about?" They're telling me, "You're dying, Frannie." Everybody is sobbing. I'm angry and swearing at them, "This is my apartment. Who are you to dare to be in my apartment?"

When I think back on it, it is like a very distorted B movie. Everything is just weird about the memory. But two things that they said got through to me.

One thing my mom said. She was sitting on the sofa crying, and I was totally detached from the situation. They were all sitting in the living room and I was sitting on the stairs in the kitchen. She said, "Fran, you know what? If we go through all this, and you get better but you never talk to me again, that will be okay." My mom and I are very close. We have a good relationship. We were born on the same day, Gemini, the twins, really similar. People who meet me know automatically that I'm her daughter. They can just tell by what I look like, and that got me. Of course, I didn't let anybody know that, but you know, I have one percent of my brain that's sane, and that got into it. So her saying that meant a lot.

The other thing that got through to me was my younger sister. We used to watch a TV show about these two little old ladies that were detectives. She and I had always talked about that, that we were going to be like them because we had always been really good friends. She said to me, "I want us to be able to be the little old ladies together, and I want our kids to be able to play with each other and be friends with each other like we have been."

Those two things got to me. I mean, besides my brother-in-law spending a lot of time talking to me, and my dad talking a lot to me. It was horrible, because, during the middle of this, I had to go into the bathroom and purge. I locked myself in the bedroom, and, oh, just horrible.

The Hardest Thing Was to Walk into Treatment

I went with them to my mom and dad's house, angry. Wrote them the nastiest letter, and didn't speak to them for three days. I don't really know the time frame here, because I'm sort of hazy about it. But I went to the treatment center for an evaluation, and the lady told me, "You're probably an alcoholic." I remember being upset about that. I said things like, "I can do outpatient eating disorder treatment." "No, not possible." I stayed at my mom and dad's house, before going into treatment. I was going to drive myself that day, and all day long I wondered, "Well, do I drive myself?" I really believed that I would not stop, probably just go straight west, California, Colorado, I don't know, but I would not stop at the treatment center. I finally decided, at the last minute, to have my mom drive me. The hardest thing I've had yet to do in this whole program, this whole time I've been in, was to walk into treatment.

My First Abstinent Day

When I was in treatment, I still purged for a while, so I've been sober about two weeks longer than I've been abstinent. I could eat breakfast, and that was all, but I was still purging. I was talking to the psychiatrist, my counselor, and my primary nurse, and I told them that I was still purging. I kept being honest with them, and they kept saying to me, "Well, you know, that is okay, you have done this for *x* amount of years, and we don't expect you to stop cold turkey." I kept telling them, and they finally said, "Okay, but from now on, when you do this, you have to bring it to community and tell people what you are doing." So I asked the whole group. I said, "I'm having trouble." One girl was just a lifesaver. She followed me around everywhere, and did not do it rudely, you know, she made a joke of it. "Let's go look at the sunset out of Frannie's room." She was just really nice. September 4, 1985, was my first abstinent day, and I've been abstinent ever since.

The Most Help: Talking Openly and Honestly

When I think about it, group was really good. Besides the time I was in college and twice with the psychiatrist, I'd never done any of this kind of stuff. The counselors were great, and community and all that stuff, but the thing that was the most helpful was just sitting around with my peers, talking. They had an eating disorder team lounge, and we'd just sit around. That's where I learned a lot about *me*. I did a lot of the major stuff, you know. In group you had to write to your eating disorder, write an eating history and drug and alcohol history, and all that kind of stuff. But, just sitting around with my friends and being able to talk openly about amounts, habits, being totally open and honest where I've never been before. Just to really get an idea of the fact that it's a disease, because I didn't believe that then, even though I was in treatment for it. I really didn't believe it. I kept saying that I eat because I want to eat, and everybody would laugh at me and say, "Well, one day you'll get it, Fran." For me, that was really helpful, just to be able to sit around with people. I liked that a lot. They had inhouse OA meetings once a week, and, it's funny, to this day, I still feel much more comfortable walking into an OA meeting than I do an AA meeting. I know that is because food is my drug of choice. I just feel much more comfortable. Maybe it's also because I know more OA people, but I know a lot of people who are dually addicted.

The Disease Concept

For me, OA is really important. I laugh about it because it's a funny name, "Overeaters Anonymous," and if you had told me a year and half ago that I would be doing a Sunday night meeting at OA, I would have laughed at you. Because, as I said, I had no clue that bulimia was compulsive overeating, and I had no clue that it was a disease. When I watched all these television shows, and I read up on it, I think it's weird, because I blocked that out, blocked the word "disease" out on all the TV shows that I watched. I'm not unintelligent, and I wouldn't have continually missed that word, the whole disease concept. Part of the disease is the feeling that it's you, that you could stop if you just had the right amount of willpower. It makes total sense, because someone who doesn't have the disease doesn't ever try to stop. They can stop, or they do stop. They don't try to stop.

So many people struggled with it when they were in treatment. They struggled with having an eating disorder. I knew I had an eating disorder. I came in for my eating disorder. A lot of people came in for drugs or alcohol and then were diagnosed as having an eating disorder. And those people struggled a lot more. Just like I've struggled more with being an alcoholic. But it's hard to say that food is your addiction when you've never in your life even been exposed to the idea that food can be an addiction. That's hard.

Breaking Away From Family

When I was in treatment, my family came whenever there was a time for the family to be there. They were there for me. They went to family recovery, a three-day thing. They came a lot. Now it's sort of hard for me because they were the only people that I was in contact with, I would say, for a good ten years. My contact with other people was sporadic; my family was my mainstay. Now I'm learning to be the independent person that I always wanted to be. And it's hard, because I still want to go back and include them in my life, but that's not realistic. I do have my own life now.

My life has changed. You know, to this day people don't comprehend. They never heard of someone who's been so close with their family. But family members were the only people I could talk to. It's sort of sad, but it's just life—a twenty-nine-old breaking away, finally. I guess, better late than never. Before, I would do anything for them. They were always the priority. I never put me first, and now I do that. Now, a meeting will come frist before a family get-together. Before, nothing came before a family function, becaust that was my responsibility as the perfect daughter.

I talk a lot about program stuff with them, but I've begun to cut back on that, because they really just want to know that I'm okay. They don't need to know all the details. They just need to know that I'm okay. One of my friends told me this, and at first I thought, "That's weird," but it's really true. I now have developed a stronger relationship with my younger sister. We talk about spiritual things; before, I never knew she was spiritual. We talk a lot about program things, and she comes to me for help, which is nice. So I've developed a different relationship with my sister. She knows that I'm still in recovery, and I'm working at it, and that's progress. My brother—I work with my brother, and he knows that. We talk a lot about program things and how to relate to a normal person's life.

Fran Is Okay Now

I really truly believe that my mom and dad think I'm better. They come up with things like, "You won't always have to go to meetings." They've gone back to old ways, and they don't remember as they did when they were in the family recovery program and they saw what a struggle I had. So now, they are not willing to go to meetings. My mom said to me one time, "Well, Fran, what do I ever do if you relapse?" I said, "Mom, that's why you go to Al-Anon." And she said, "Well, I only have about six questions. I don't want to go to Al-Anon just for six questions." Well, that's okay, because they are my parents, and they're not my life, you know. I hope I never relapse. That is why I would want them to be involved, but they're not, and that is okay. They're busy, and their life goes on, and Fran is okay. So the worry isn't there anymore. My mom told me that this is the first time in ten years that she does not know my phone number or address. That's never happened to her before.

Dating—Not Yet

After treatment, you're not supposed to date for a year, and I didn't. I am sober and abstinent for more than a year now. But that whole idea makes me sort of scared, because everybody I know, who gets into a relationship, who has not spent a lot of time on themselves, gets messed up. They relapse, and they eat flour, sugar, purge, drink, whatever. For me, the major thing that I work on still is my low self-esteem, my self-acceptance. If I can find a guy who gives me that, I'm not going to do any work on me. So, as a result, and I truly believe this, if I ever get into a relationship, it probably will be with someone who is in recovery like I am. Then I won't have to go to him to be validated. I would be validated by my own process.

Change Is Possible

It is frightening to change. The idea of open and honest communication is so totally different from the way it was before. Before, every time I went into a social situation, I was terrified. I had to drink to make myself feel better and then I had to drink to just walk into the room. I had those fears then of rejection and judgment, and all that. I felt that if I said to one of those friends, or a guy I was dating, or whatever, "This is how I'm afraid of life and people," they would think I was crazy. But now it's really different. A year ago, I had been out of treatment for a couple weeks and went to the Halloween dance they had at the halfway house, and I couldn't do anything. All I could do is go and sit. I was totally uncomfortable at the first one.

This year I went—now think of this, an eating disorder person! I wore a leotard and a tutu, and I danced! Every single person I talked to, I said, "I'm very afraid, and I'm nervous to be dancing," and everybody helped me. Every single person was supportive and told me different things that helped them get through their first dance, sober and abstinent. Now I can talk to anybody about almost anything; about my fears, about my successes, and not sound grandiose. If I'm being honest, if I'm just plain old being honest, then I'm going to be okay. I've never had that before. When I look back at my friends in high school, it was nothing like the communication I have with people today. It's just plain old honesty, that's all.

The Happiest I Have Ever Been

Everything has changed. As a result of being sober and abstinent, I may not have a great paying job, but I have a good paying job. I was able to buy a new car; move to a new apartment. I haven't been overdrawn once; I pay my bills on time. I'm capable of learning, and I'm capable of helping other people learn. It's fun. And that's the thing I like. I mean, I may be weird, but I have fun now.

To somebody who has an eating disorder, I would say, it's just really simple. You don't have to live like that. You do have an option. I felt that I had no choice whatsoever. I was afraid of what I would do without my eating behavior. But, you know, I am the happiest I have ever been. When I turned twenty-nine last summer, it was the first time in ten years that I was not afraid to get older. This was the first time I felt okay to be alive. It's just really simple. You don't have to live like that.

Preface to Amy

*C*ross-addiction with food and alcohol was a problem for Dave, Jennifer, and Frannie. With Amy, the cross-addiction also involves the habitual use of amphetamines starting at the age of thirteen.

The stereotype of the fresh-faced, healthy athlete is shattered by Amy's story. The eating disorder presented early, in grade school. She remembers turning to food whenever she was upset. Her occasional use of alcohol as a child gave her a feeling of numbness that she liked, a feeling she also got from her eating. At age thirteen, she began using amphetamines and vomiting to lose weight for gymnastics in a cycle of starvation alternating with binging and purging. The emphasis on the body that is a normal part of athletics only accelerated her already established eating disorder. "I can remember my coaches always telling me that I was fat, and 'you gotta lose weight, you gotta lose weight.'" Today, she is a frequent speaker at parent groups, telling them that good kids, athletes, can and do end up with alcoholism, drug addiction, and eating disorders. Amy is lucky—she is recovering.

Before she recovered, her bulimia and alcohol and drug addiction pushed her to an attempted suicide in college. Fortunately, it got her into treatment, first for alcoholism, then for her eating illness. Her story emphatically points out the need for concurrent treatment of cross-addiction.

After she stopped drinking, she still binged, then started starving, and inevitably began craving amphetamines again as part of the old familiar cycle. In all probability, she would have lost her sobriety as well if the process had continued. By entering an eating disorder treatment program concurrent with her alcohol treatment, she was able to address the other part of her addictive behavior, and begin recovery.

Amy had to deal with a serious trauma that surfaced during her alcohol treatment. As a teenager, she was raped when she got drunk and blacked out one New Year's Eve. Before treatment, she had no memory of that event. When she began to remember during treatment, she sought counseling for it. It is interesting to note her own response to this trauma that only recently became part of her consciousness: she says it is a "pretty new issue" for her, and that she's "still trying to cope with it." The point to be made here is that she is abstinent and in recovery, regardless of *other* unresolved problems or traumas in her life. And she is clearly enjoying her new freedom. As she says at the end, "My life is real neat now."

AMY

Always Self-Conscious about My Body

My eating disorder started when I was really, young, probably about five. My parents weren't home a lot, and I was really self-sufficient then, or so I thought. I have an older brother and sister who are ten and eleven years older than I, so I was pretty much like an only child. I can remember coming home from kindergarten and sitting in front of the TV and eating bags of potato chips with ketchup on them. And I was always a candy fanatic, constantly eating candy.

Since my sister was so much older than I was, she was already into what her body looked like, so I thought I had to be, too. My mom is kind of heavy, and I didn't want to look like my mom. From an early age, I can always remember thinking, "I'm not going to get fat; I'm always going to be thin." I can remember my sister looking in the mirror and saying, "God, I hate my thighs," and things like that. So, early on, I was looking in the mirror and saying, "God, I hate my thighs, I hate my chest." I was about seven years old—I didn't have a chest. I didn't even have thighs at that time. But I can always remember being really self-conscious about my body.

I Had to Hold My Family Together

I always felt inferior to people, too, because I was short. So I overcompensated. I was real cocky. I beat up a lot of people to prove that even though I was short, I wasn't inferior. I think a lot of my behaviors were always fearful. My family used to fight a lot, especially my mother and father; I can remember running and hiding in my bedroom and crying.

My mom has a lot of emotional problems. She tried to commit suicide when I was younger. She's not really stable, that's always bothered me. She has always been what I consider weak. My father, though, was always so strong, like a brick wall, and that bothered the hell out of me. My mom used to hate it.

I've always loved my sister and I've always hated her, because I've always taken care of her. I was like the big sister, even though she's about ten years older. I was always there to get her out of jams when I was a little girl. She'd come in with problems, and we'd talk them through.

I always felt I was looking after my parents, too. My mother and my father would fight and I would tell them, "You go in that room, and you go in this room. Until you guys calm down, I want you in your rooms." I was about ten and telling my parents to go into their bedrooms. I always did that. When I was in treatment we had a family counseling session and it was the same. They came in and I said, "Mom, you sit there, Dad you sit there." My sister was there, and I said, "Sis, you sit there." I had my little nephew, and I said, "Nephew, you sit in my lap. I don't want anyone talking until you are told to," and they all sat there and didn't say a thing.

It was a really big responsibility. I had to hold my family together, or so I thought, because my family always thought that I had myself together.

Family Denial

A big part of my family is non-confrontation, a really big part. I think that I can joke about it now, but who wants to confront it when you have all these problems? We'll sweep it under the rug and think it will be okay. That didn't work. It's taken a toll on the family. Now I'm dragging things out of those guys, starting to make them talk about what's happened with me and what's happened with my sister. I find a lot of denial, but they're starting to get better. A lot of denial—with me, with my sister, with themselves. It's just that really addictive personality. My father's an alcoholic who doesn't drink. He's never been a drinker, but he has the personality of an alcoholic.

There was quite a lot of verbal abuse from my dad. He is very much a perfectionist. My mom is not. She makes mistakes. My dad couldn't stand that in any of us. He always wanted us to be perfect, like him. I can remember trying to be perfect at my sports and my schoolwork.

Anything that I did, if I didn't do it perfectly, I didn't want to do it at all.

I got a lot of mixed signals from my parents: "Whatever you want to be, kid, we will support you, but you have to make money, you have to be successful, and this, and this, and this. But, whatever you do, we will support you." I was always really confused with that, with what they wanted of me. So, growing up, I always did what they wanted, not what I wanted, but what Mom and Dad wanted. I picked my boyfriends because of what my parents wanted them to be, to have a good background. I finally rebelled against that completely and went with guys who were the scum of the earth, just to get back at my parents.

I Was Always Turning to Food

My eating disorder really set in when I was in the eighth grade. My brother died—he was kind of like an adopted brother. He was my brother's best friend and his parents had died, so my parents took him in. I was so young. I knew he wasn't a blood relative, but he was my brother. That's how he was introduced, as my brother. And then, when he died, when I was in eighth grade, no one would talk about it, no one told me. They just said Paul had died, and that was it. I can remember running and stealing money from my parents, and going to a candy store and buying all this candy, and sitting and just eating all this food. That's probably my first real remembrance of a really big binge, feeling sick and making myself throw up. That's the first time I ever made myself throw up. When I was really upset, I was always turning to food. At that point I hadn't found alcohol and drugs. I was really concentrating on food a lot.

I took my first drink when I was eight, because my brother and sister babysat me, and they used to give me little beers so I wouldn't tell Mom and Dad that they were having a party or something. I would drink them and pass out, and they would put me to bed. That was really convenient for them, and I thought I was cool, because I was hanging around with all the older kids.

But I didn't drink on a regular basis, only when my brother and sister had parties. But I can remember that feeling. That's what the food did, too—the numbness, the feeling that everything is okay now. Except when I would wake up the next morning and feel tremendously fat, and really sick.

Something else that transpired through my growing up years is that I didn't like people my age, I thought they were young and immature. I liked my brother's and sister's friends, I hung around with them a lot. I was like everyone's little sister. Always, again, feeling I was better than everybody else my age—thinking, "These kids, they don't know anything." I was the egomaniac with the inferiority complex. That's me—completely!

Purging and Amphetamines at Thirteen

When I was thirteen, purging started to be an everyday thing because I liked my food, I liked eating a lot, but I didn't want to gain that weight. I started getting into gymnastics around that time, too. Again, there, your body image is so important. I can remember my coaches always telling me that I was fat. "You gotta' lose weight. You gotta' lose weight." I was about 100 pounds—I wasn't fat! I can remember everyone else telling me, "If you don't watch it, Amy, you're going to have thighs like your sister and your mom." That was the big family joke, we got the fat side of my grandparents, you know—"thunder-thighs." I would just cringe at that. I did have pretty big thighs. They were muscled, but in my eyes they were all fat. That's when a lot of my eating disorder really, really super kicked in.

I would starve, and starve, and starve. I started using speed at the time to help me starve. That's when my drug addiction and my eating disorders all became one and the same, because I used my drugs to help me starve and control my eating habits. I was using speed regularly, and I was wired. I'm hyper to begin with, and then, on speed, I was just bouncing off the walls. I could go three or four days without eating; just drinking water. Then after that I'd be so hungry, I would binge for two or three days. It would be nonstop eat and purge, eat and purge, eat and purge. I can remember going into restaurants with boyfriends and purging. It got so bad, at the end, that when I would take water, I would have to throw it up. Anything that would go down my throat caused an automatic reaction. I didn't have to force it, I could do it mentally. I can remember, in high school, doing reports and term papers on eating disorders, and thinking, "I'll never have one," and *knowing* I had one. Maybe what I thought was, "I'll write these papers, and someone will see something." A lot of my friends had anorexia or similar things, and I had tried helping them, I think in the back of my mind hoping that someone would help me. But I was too secretive about it. No one did help.

I started getting speed from my brother-in-law. My sister was on it, my mom was on it, and I was on it. It was from a black-market doctor, and it was shipped from the clinic. My mom would buy a bottle, and I would buy a bottle. She would steal some from me, and I would steal some from her when I'd run out. My family, my whole family, has an eating disorder. My mother is a compulsive overeater, and my sister is severely anorexic. It was really convenient having the whole family with eating disorders living together, because no one was going to say anything to someone else about taking the speed.

In College, Sick from Speed and Purging

The speed really got out of hand during my freshman year at college. My girlfriends at college would hide it, and I would go out and buy over-the-counter stimulants, or whatever I could get, and drink caffeine. I would have to drink cases of soft drinks with caffeine in them, and I would have to keep chugging them with a couple of bottles of stimulants. Or they would find my drug supplier, and they would tell him, "Don't sell any more speed to Amy," and I would have to find another one. I had a friend whose brother worked at a clinic, and he got speed for us. It was really good speed. I was taking about ten to fifteen hits a day. I was physically sick all the time, because it was running my body down.

Also at this time, the vomiting was taking a toll. I started to get preulcers, and my teeth were all rotting away. People would stay with me at meals so I wouldn't throw up, but I would always find a way to do it. This is the most disgusting part: just to vomit (for some reason I liked that ritual), I would find food in garbage cans, like old pizza, or something, wipe it clean, eat it, and then vomit. All that, just so I could get that vomit in. I would have to do that if I didn't have food in my dorm or if the cafeteria was closed. A lot of times that was at night.

After I vomited, I felt relief—it was like a high, almost. My head would be kind of light; I would feel empty. That was what I liked. I liked that empty feeling.

After a While, It Didn't Work for Me Anymore

I would get anxious if I couldn't vomit. I would always be trying to find an excuse to do it, and was really preoccupied: "Where am I going to throw up? Where am I going to do it?" A lot of my fun was ruined by that, because we'd eat and I'd be always looking around. People thought I was paranoid, because I was looking all the time just to find a place. If I had to, I'd go out and find bushes and throw up there. I liked the preoccupation of vomiting. And I liked the feeling afterwards.

But then, around the end of my freshman year in college, I didn't like it anymore. I wasn't getting high, I wasn't feeling empty, yet I was continuously doing it. I would just continuously eat to throw up, to feel that way again, but it wasn't happening. That was getting really scary for me, because I knew something was wrong. Of course, I had known something was wrong all along; I didn't think normal people did this.

My weight was always normal, just normal. Right on the charts, not under, not over. But at that time, I started gaining weight. My freshman year at college. That "freshman fifteen" that they all talk about, I got that. I was flipping out, and my clothes wouldn't fit me anymore. I wouldn't go clothes shopping because I wasn't the size I thought I was supposed to be. I can remember my fiancé and me shopping, and me just hysterically crying after we got out of there. He was saying, "What the hell is wrong with you?" "I can't wear any clothes." I was screaming and crying hysterically about the whole thing, weighing myself continuously, trying to lose weight, and I couldn't lose it anymore. My starving had left me. I was incapable of starving because the speed wasn't doing what it used to do anymore.

Fat and Suicidal

I couldn't starve anymore. I kept putting on weight because my vomiting had turned on me. It wasn't helping me maintain or lose weight either, and I started gaining, gaining, gaining. I was 160 pounds, and I flipped out. I was looking at myself in the mirror and seeing this huge, obese person. At that time my boyfriend was going to break up with me, and I couldn't handle that, and I couldn't handle being fat, so I tried to kill myself. This was in the middle of my sophomore year.

You know, drinking was never my big thing. I didn't like to drink because I was really out of control when I did it, because I'd get drunk, and I'd get sick. That didn't turn me on. But in college drinking was starting to become a problem. I was starting to get to the problem drinking stage. If I would have continued on that path, I think the true alcoholism would have come in really quick. I'm an alcoholic only because I was on that road.

I thought, if I come home and go to another school, then I'll be okay and everything will be better. I'd be close to my boyfriend and be close to my parents, and I'll be okay then. I transferred to another school, but it didn't happen. My roommates were users, and I started to get high a lot on pot.

Also, I used cocaine periodically. I liked the high it gave me, and that seemed to take over what the speed wasn't doing anymore, with the noneating. I kind of liked that, but I could never afford it, so I would only get it when someone would give it to me or something.

The Psychiatrist Didn't Help

It seemed like the progression of the disease was getting worse and worse. At that time I started seeing a psychiatrist. At the end of my freshman year, one of my teachers told me I was an addict and got me to see a counselor. The counselor called my parents, and told my parents that, yes, I was a drug addict, and that I needed treatment. He had suggested a good treatment center. My parents' response was, "No way, not my baby. She is wonderful, she is great, and she doesn't do anything wrong." They said, "We're just going to let her see a psychiatrist for a while." So, that's what I did. I came home that summer and started seeing him. My parents, my brother, and my sister all saw him.

This guy was so stupid that I conned the hell out of him. He didn't know about the eating disorder disease. He had not a clue as to what it was. We tried hypnosis, and I'd get high right after I left. I'd be on speed while I was there. He'd try hypnosis for the food, too, and the vomiting, and it never worked. I'd come back and say, "Oh, God, it worked. It was great. Man, you're really doing it," and inside I'm saying, "You're a jerk. My parents are paying you 120 bucks an hour, and you're not doing squat." But I wasn't going to let anyone know that, because I was afraid they might put me into treatment. So, I went back to using, and eating, and all that again. When I tried to commit suicide, I had just dropped out, about a month or two before. Now I told him that I was well, that I was all done with this whole thing. He agreed with me.

Suicide Seemed Like the Only Answer

Nothing in particular triggered my suicide attempt. I think it was just an accumulation of everything. My boyfriend wanted to leave me. We had been dating at that time for three and a half, maybe four years. That was hard. The whole body image, the way I was seeing myself, was getting out of hand. I was starting to fall out of school, because all I did was sit in my dorm room and drink and do drugs. I didn't care about doing anything, didn't care about my hygiene. I would go to bars in slacks and my hair not done, in an old T-shirt, just really punky, just to get some drugs. That's it; that's all I wanted. That and to be with my boyfriend. I had no friends. I had people who cared about me, but I put them out of my mind. I didn't want them there. I didn't want anyone to care about me, because I knew that I was going to try to commit suicide. I knew I was at that point. A lot of my suicide attempt was for attention, to get help, because I knew I had a problem. I knew that if I went to my parents and asked for help, nothing would be done, I would be slapped back to the family shrink, and it would have been the same old thing.

It was a big ploy for help, and then, after I did it, I thought, "Oh, no, why did I do it?" Because I was afraid to get help. I can remember calling my boyfriend that night after taking all the pills, and telling him I tried to commit suicide and his saying, "No, you didn't—you're a liar. You're just doing this to get me back," and on, and on, and on. He hung up the phone on me. That didn't work, so I went to bed, and I woke up about four in the morning, sicker than a dog, vomiting blood. Just at that point I thought, "This is it, my God, I'm going to die."

I called the hospital, because it's right down the street from the school, and I said, "I just tried to kill myself, and I'm going to die, and I'm afraid." They said, "Okay, where are you? Can you get here, or do you want us to send an ambulance?" I thought, "Oh, great, people are going to wake up and see all this," and I didn't want people to know. So I got two of my friends up, and they rushed me to the hospital. It was on April Fool's Day. They called my parents and told my parents to come down immediately. They got hold of my boyfriend and he came down. Everyone was flipped out. Everyone was yelling at me, screaming at me, "You son-of-a-bitch, how can you do this to us?" And on, and on, and on. I was still flipped out that I was going to die, so I really didn't pay much attention to that. The way I deal with pain a lot of time is, I laugh and joke. The whole time I'm in there, I'm laughing about this thing, and throwing up all over the place, and laughing and making jokes with the nurses. They didn't think I was really funny, you know. But I couldn't deal with the pain I was feeling. I didn't cry about it the whole time those people were around.

Another Attempt at Treatment—For Alcoholism

They put me in the psych ward, and my parents didn't like the doctor I had. He had a really bad reputation, so they got me out of there, through the courts, I think. I'm not sure how they got me out, but I think, since I was a suicide, you're not allowed to be out unless you have signed permission or something from a doctor. So I got transferred to another hospital and stayed in their psych ward for about four days. They told me, "You're not crazy, you're an alcoholic." I said, "I'm not an alcoholic. How do you get that from a suicide attempt?" I couldn't figure out how they did it. To this day I can't figure out how they knew that I was an alcoholic.

They asked me questions like, do I drink? "Yeah." Do I do drugs? I said, "Well, a little." They asked me if I ever had a blackout. I told them I didn't believe people had blackouts, that it was their mind putting away something stupid that they did so they couldn't remember. When I went into treatment, they all called me the blackout person. I got a reputation over that.

Remembering a Rape

They put me over into treatment, and that's when things started happening. I started realizing that I was an addict, but I was still binging and purging. It was really convenient, because they fed you a lot of sugar to get you off the booze, and that was great. I was in seventh heaven, but meanwhile, still gaining more and more weight. I worked through a lot of neat things there. I have a really special place in my heart for that place, I guess because I got sober there. They really dug through some other underlying issues that I had never dealt with—a rape that happened when I was younger. It came out. I don't even know how the hell it came up because I didn't remember it. It just, like, popped out. They dealt with that with me, and that was really neat.

I had been raped by a boyfriend. Actually, by a boyfriend and his seven friends. It happened when I was fifteen, I think. It was on New Year's Eve, and I was drunk and in a blackout, so I can only remember bits and parts and pieces of waking up to it. They stumbled on this in treatment. Because I'm really flirtatious with people, a guy in treatment said something to me off-the-wall about a new guy who came in. It was something really stupid, insinuating that he thought I was a slut, and I just flew. I slapped the hell out of him, and I remember running into my counselor's office screaming about this rape. I don't know where it came from, and I don't know what happened. Previously I had had some nightmares, which were really frequent. I had a lot of nightmares about it, because I didn't tell anybody. I never told anyone about it until that time in treatment. That was the first time I had ever told anyone. Dealing with the rape was really hard, because that was a big loss of control for me. I think that was one of the reasons I have to deal with it.

I Deal with It Little by Little

I blocked it out really well, but little things have come back to me. At first it was just the rape I had by my boyfriend, and then I remembered other parts of it. Then I'd remember a little more; then a little more. I don't know what will happen in the future, if the whole thing will be clear to me, unless God sees fit that I'm ready to deal with more. That seems to be what it is: God seems to think that I can deal with a little more, so He gives me something, just a little more, to deal with. As I said, I felt completely out of control, and right after it happened I got really sick and almost died. It was mono that I had, and I ended up in intensive care for a long time, in isolation. I was in the hospital six weeks, starting two weeks after the rape.

I was in medical journals, because none of the doctors could figure out what the hell was wrong with me. All that came up was that I had mono. They were going to have to do a tracheotomy once, because I stopped breathing. I wonder if that was my way of trying to kill myself. I wanted to die. But I didn't.

My parents found out about it just a couple months ago. I told them about it. And my mom said, "Well, couldn't you come and talk to us?" I couldn't. At that point I felt I was so bad that I couldn't talk to anyone. The guy who did it is really sick—he is a really sick man. He has a problem, bad problems. For that I can excuse him—for the action, I can't. That was a long, hard thing for me to deal with—still is—trying to cope with it. It's pretty new, a pretty new issue for me. But I've seen some counselors for it.

Finally, Diagnosis of an Eating Disorder

The treatment program in that first center was usually twenty-one days, but I begged them to not let me go after twenty-one days. I didn't want to leave. I didn't think I was ready, I was afraid I would go back out there. So I stayed another week and went into a halfway house. They did the interview for the halfway house, and they asked me if I ever vomited after I ate. I said, "Sure," as if everyone did this. And they slapped me in an eating disorder group. I was just two months into sobriety, and all these people in the group had gone through treatment for an eating disorder and I hadn't. I didn't understand what the hell an eating disorder was. I didn't know how to help an eating disorder. I kept going to their groups, and I stopped vomiting at that time, but I kept binge eating. Then I started starving and started getting really bad. I wanted to go back to using my speed.

That's when a counselor said, "That's it. You're going into treatment again. You've got to get help." I did want to go, but I was a little afraid of it. I told my parents that I needed help again; they weren't really pleased about it, but I went in, no matter. At that point, a little bit of some sobriety was starting to rub off. I just had ninety days, and I saw that I was going to lose it again, with my eating disorder, if I didn't get help.

I Still Wasn't Ready for Help

But when I went to eating disorder treatment, I still wasn't really ready for help. I binge ate my way through treatment. I think I was abstinent a couple of days in there, but I was not truly abstinent. Again, it was just . . . I was too afraid to give that up. I wasn't vomiting; I had given that up when I went in treatment. That was the last time I had vomited. I was just binge eating, not even starving any more. It wasn't even really big binges. They were—actually, I don't even know if they were binges—they were just not following the program. I'd have a candy bar here, and a candy bar there. I wasn't being honest in treatment.

Three weeks into my treatment they found out. They caught my dishonesty, although still not knowing that I was binge eating or eating the sugar. I started getting a little more honest. My sugar use lessened, and that's when I started getting a couple days' abstinence here and a day there. But I can remember the doctor telling people, the newcomers, "Go talk to Amy, because she's really doing well. She's really working." I was conning them, too. I wanted someone to see through it, but no one was. That made me mad, because I wasn't capable of being honest. I thought I was one of those who are constitutionally incapable of being honest.

In the first treatment program, I was diagnosed as manic depressive. I never believed that. That was my eating disorder. When I got into treatment for an eating disorder, they took me off the lithium and I haven't had a mood swing since I became abstinent. I really believe that manic depression was induced by my eating—it was all sugar-related.

Starting to be Abstinent

My eating disorder treatment didn't really start to work until about three weeks after I got out of treatment. I had just moved into the halfway house. About my third day back there, I went into a temper tantrum. I was going to go out and drink, and eat, and to hell with everything. I was with two of my girlfriends. We were going to go out and get bombed that night. They went out and got drunk, but I stayed at the halfway house for some reason— maybe divine intervention. They're still out there. After that temper tantrum is when I started to be honest and work on being abstinent.

There was a counselor and about twelve or fifteen girls in my group. Sick people, a lot of people like me who weren't sure whether or not they wanted to give it up. We met as a group every day with the counselor, and we had individual counseling every week. The neat thing is that once I started getting well, I still wasn't going to the OA or AA meetings, but I started becoming abstinent. At that time I hated AA meetings and I hated OA meetings. Once in a blue moon I would go.

Getting Serious About Getting Better

Then, last December, I hit bottom again, emotionally. My life was unmanageable. I hated myself. Then I started going to AA and OA meetings, and found a sponsor. I also broke up with my boyfriend. We had still been going out through all this, on and off. The counselors had said, "You've got to break up with him, because he is still using." He was still using pot and acid, and was drinking. We had dated for six years. It was really hard to give up, especially since he was my last addiction. I wasn't really willing to give him up, but I finally did, and that was really neat.

When I started going to meetings, I unfortunately got hooked up into an OA group that had their OA status taken away from them because, I believe, they were a cult. They were very controlling people. They told me I wasn't an alcoholic, that it was just my compulsive overeating, and that I could go back to drinking any time. At that point, I wasn't really stable with my alcoholism, and I thought, "Wow, I wonder if I can?" Then I started talking to people about it, and I got the hell out of there.

Food Doesn't Cause a Problem Anymore

Now I have a real good OA group. We only meet once a week, but I started learning how to work a Twelve Step program. It's nice meeting once a week with the women I love. A couple of them are my grandsponsors, and they're my best friends. Food doesn't cause a problem in my life anymore. That is the biggest miracle that I can ever think of that God has given me.

I don't know what happened. It just started happening. I had a candy bar about seven, eight months ago, and it was a joke. I had this half a candy bar, and I said, "Hey, I ate a stupid candy bar." They said, "Did it help?" and I said, "No, it didn't even taste good." I threw it out, after eating only half of it. It was not doing anything for me any more.

Before now, I never knew how to have a relationship with someone. Now, most definitely, my friends have replaced my addictions. That's really positive. I needed to have something to replace my addictions. And I do a lot of service work. You know, I don't have time to drink anymore. When I start hanging out with some recovering people, some of the winners, that's when I started being abstinent. My abstinence became a lot easier.

I'm really active in OA, and I speak a lot to high school students and athletes. I speak to parent groups, to tell them that good kids do end up with alcoholism and drug addiction. You know, I was in student government, cheerleading, gymnastics, orchestra, theater. I worked in the office. My parents are very respected people in the community. I always dressed well. I was the last person anyone ever thought would have a problem.

My Friends from Recovery Are My Family Now

My relationship with my family has changed too. I had to pull away from them, because it was a really unhealthy dependency with my mom and dad. The rest of my family still has it, my brother and sister, and I pulled away from them. I'm living at home now, and it's really hard. I love my parents dearly, they're great people, and they've done the best with me that they could, but I just don't *like* them. I see a lot of the old me in them, and I don't like that part anymore. I don't like to be staring at it all the time.

The relationship with my father has developed. My dad and I love each other, which we never did when I was growing up—we always hated each other. I'm very much like my father, *very* much like my father, and he didn't like me and I didn't like him. Today, my dad's the one I'm close to, not my mom. When I was younger, it was always my mom and I who were close. She was my best friend. Now my mom and I have a lot of problems, and my dad and I are really close. He tells me how much he respects me, which is like, wow, he's never said that to me before.

My friends from OA and from treatment are like my family now. And it's neat, because I finally have a healthy family. I cling to them really hard. My mom doesn't like that. She gets jealous sometimes because I don't go to her with my problems. I'm not comfortable going to my mom—she doesn't know anything about recovery.

Today I Enjoy Living

I try not to think about the future too much, because it can be really overwhelming. When I was in my worst period, that's all I did. I had my life down on paper—where I was going to work when I got out of college, the date I was going to get married, what my wedding was going to be like, what kind of house, how my apartment was going to be decorated, what year I was going to have my first child, and all that. I used to write it on paper, and cross things out, change them. I was so obsessed with the future.

My life is really neat now. I enjoy living, which I have never done before. I've always wanted to die; I don't want to die anymore. That's another miracle—not just that I'm sober and abstinent, but I don't have suicidal thoughts anymore. I'm really grateful.

All that's because of my fellowships and, most of all, because of my Higher Power. You know, all the divine interventions are no coincidence, which I thought they were. My Higher Power has always given me exactly what I've needed, when I've needed it. I started becoming aware of that not too long ago. This whole God issue is really hard for me. I used to think AA was a cult. But when I started really praying, and things were coming true, and my life was getting better, then I had to take a good look. And now I think—this isn't just me doing it anymore!

Preface to Pat

*P*at came from a nice, ordinary family. She worked hard, made a good salary, and after her divorce she lived at home with her parents. But she was always broke, and she wanted to die. Why?

Pat was an addict. Starting in her childhood, her primary addiction was food, but by the time she got to treatment it was food, alcohol, and heroin. Her heroin addiction might seem shocking to some, although fifteen years ago, cocaine, now a common middle-class drug of abuse, was also considered to be outside the mainstream. Put in this perspective, Pat's story is not very much of a departure from the other histories of cross-addiction in this book. Whereas the circumstances of her life made alcohol, amphetamines, and food drugs of convenience for Amy, the circumstances of Pat's life made alcohol, heroin, and food her addictions.

From Pat's point of veiw, "They are all similar and they all do the same thing." She feels that if she ever starts to believe that "it's okay to pick up food instead of picking up a drug," then "it will lead me right back to drugs. I guess the most important thing I learned through treatment is that this disease [eating disorder] is going to kill me if I don't take care of myself. It's just as severe as alcohol or drug addiction and it's probably my primary disease."

Pat's story, and the phenomenon of cross-addiction, raise provocative questions about the nature of addiction. Is it just one disease with many manifestations? How does her food addiction differ from her alcohol or heroin addiction? Looking at it objectively, ignoring any social or moral stigma attached to the drug, is her heroin addiction any different from her food addiction, when judged in terms of the damage it inflicts on the individual user? What are the implications for causality and treatment? Those questions cannot be answered here, but should be asked if eating illnesses are ever to be understood. As Pat says, "People don't understand." Her story should help to increase the understanding.

PAT

I Hit Bottom on Heroin

Besides having an eating disorder, I'm also an addict and an alcoholic, and I hit bottom. I was using heroin. It was the last drug I was using. I hit bottom on the heroin, and I really, honestly, don't know how I recovered except for God's grace. When I was hitting bottom in my last year and a half of using, I would hang out down on the south side of the city. I would drive on the expressways to go to work in the morning, and this particular morning, I nodded out behind the wheel, and I woke up almost underneath a semi. I knew that I had two choices: one, to go to treatment; or, two, to die.

I remembered that a few years ago my uncle went through treatment. I went to work, and I looked up the phone number. It was a place that specializes in cross-addiction. I called, and I hung up. But there was something driving me. I asked a guy I worked with, who knew I had a problem, to call for me. He did, and by twelve o'clock that day I was checked in as an inpatient.

Alcoholism and Eating Disorder

I was evaluated when I walked in. I knew for sure I was a drug addict. I didn't know I was an alcoholic, and I didn't know I had an eating disorder. I guess I must have been at detox a day or two when the nurses came in and presented me with that idea. I said, "No, no, no. I don't have an eating disorder." But they sat on the bed and explained to me what an eating disorder is. What it involved, the symptoms— losing weight and gaining it back. Losing more than ten pounds and gaining back more. They felt that if I would not be treated for this eating disorder, that I would go back out and use. That scared me, because I knew I would die if I did that. Everything they said—I don't remember much because I was in detox—just hit, and everything applied to what had gone on with my whole life. Then they asked me if I would be willing to go to the eating disorder team, and I agreed. I went into detox for four or five days, then I went to the eating disorder team. The funny thing is that when I went into treatment, I remember consciously thinking that if I went into treatment then I wouldn't be spending all this money on my drugs, so I could use the money to go to the fat doctor, and get prescriptions for speed from him, so I could lose weight. That's how sick my thinking was.

Food Was Like Another Drug

This particular eating disorder program is for dually addicted people, so they dealt with my addiction, with my alcoholism (which I was not aware of when I went in), and with my eating disorder, too. It took them longer to get me to admit I was an alcoholic than it did for them to get me to admit I had an eating disorder. But they dealt with all of that. And when I look back at my life, all of it is the same.

When I was in treatment, I did a food history and an alcohol and drug history, so I was dealing with all of them at the same time. This was good for me because, as I said, I started out on food and then I found alcohol. When I found alcohol, I started losing weight because I was replacing the food with alcohol, and then I went back to food. And then I found speed and downers, but I would go back to the food, and then I found cocaine, and at the end it was heroin and food, both of them. I couldn't stop the feelings that I was trying to stuff, so I was using anything I could. The funny thing is, when most people use heroin they lose a lot of weight, but I was gaining. Because I was using the food as much as the drug, food was just another drug.

I Always Had an Eating Disorder

Looking back, I can see that I always had the characteristics of an eating disorder—the feelings of inadequacy, the feelings of never being a part of things, always thinking if I was thnner I'd be accepted or that my physical appearance was why I was not accepted. I can go back to about third grade, maybe even before that, even first and second grade. Leaving for school, I would be so fearful of going to school and being around other people that I would hide underneath the windowsill by the kitchen and watch the bus drive by so I could tell my mom I missed the bus and wouldn't have to go. I never felt a part of things in school. My mom and I have done a lot of sharing since I have come into the program. One thing that she said is, she would go to school for a parent conference or something and tell the teachers that she was my mother, and they would say, "Oh, Pat, she doesn't talk too much. We really don't know anything about her." I was always in the background. I would never want anyone to know anything about me. I think it was always very hard for me to have more than one friend at a time. I don't think I ever did.

I'm the oldest of four. I have two brothers and a sister. Another thing I discovered in my thinking is, I always felt my dad wanted me to be a boy. That, too, made me feel like I was not what I was supposed to be. I was not good enough, not accepted. I was fearful of my father, very fearful of him. I remember being afraid to be with my dad, and I remember being close with my mother.

It Got Really Bad in Junior High School

Part of the disease is these feelings of not being a part of things, of always being overweight, always thinking I was not cute, and not being able to live up to what other people expected of me. This goes as far back as I can remember. There's not a particular time when I can say, "Yes, this is where it happened." It started progressing, and it started getting really bad when I was in junior high. The disease really started before that. I would steal money from my dad when I was in fourth, fifth, and sixth grade. His wallet would be on the counter, and I would steal money for candy. Or I would steal pop bottles and return them to buy candy. As long as I had that, I was okay. I didn't need friends. But when I was in junior high, seventh or eighth grade, the feelings of being left out were very strong. I was always trying and not making it, trying out for cheerleading and for the basketball team and the chorus, and just feeling like a complete failure, not being one of the "in crowd." And that affected me a lot. A lot.

High School—Drinking for Confidence

Up to the point of going into high school I was only a compulsive overeater. My bulimia and drinking came in when I was in high school. When I was a freshman, I had two friends. One of them had been my friend since I was about three years old, the only friend I could ever keep, because I was not a nice person. She was my friend in high school, she and another girl, a relative of mine. We were always together, and one time (I remember this vividly because I'm an alcoholic, and alcoholics remember drinking stories) she was going out with a senior football player, and she was accepted by everyone. She was "okay." They would go out and get drunk, and I set my mind to it, I wanted to know what this was about. I was very naive, I didn't know anything about anything. I had not had a boyfriend. I wanted to find out what getting drunk was all about, and so we went to her house. There was a bottle of liquor and some beer there. Her boyfriend was supposed to show up, but he was late. So I manipulated and conned her to start drinking before he got there, even though she didn't want to. By the time he got there we had finished the bottle of liquor and some beer, and we were both in a cloud.

For the first time, I was able to talk around his friends. I was able to flirt. I felt accepted. I felt people were laughing *with* me instead of *at* me, when really they were still laughing at me like they had done my whole life. It was like love, and I was off and running. I lost that closeness with my friend because now it was, "I want to drink," and "I want to get drunk," and "I want to be with people who drink." I started hanging around with a girl who was really experienced in everything that I knew nothing about, like drinking and drugging and sex, and all that, and she became my best friend. She also introduced me to a boy.

Uppers and Downers

It seemed that using speed was good because then I could lose weight. If I took speed, I wouldn't have to eat. So I would take speed during the day, and I wouldn't eat. And I lost weight. I never felt that accepted feeling again, but I figured, well, if I keep losing weight, then this is working, so I'll do more. I was having money problems because I was drinking and everything was costing so much. Then I got introduced to downers, so I was taking speed during the day and downers at night, and I was up, down, up, down, up, down.

I worked all through school so I could pay for my addictions. I started working as a summer camp counselor, and I worked all through high school. I still couldn't make enough money, so I started working at a shoe store, selling handbags, working on commission. I was the best salesperson they had. They couldn't figure out why. I knew the only way I could get drugs and food was to sell, so I was good at sales. I would also steal money from my mom and dad.

Hunger Pain Was Good

There's something I just remembered this week. I don't really know at what point in my life this really happened, but I was young. I think my dad said this to me (my mom said she said it, but I recall it as my dad), that a doctor told him, "when you feel hunger pain, it's okay, that's good, because that means your body is eating your fat." So all through high school, when I was doing these drugs and was more or less starving myself, I felt it was okay. Because the hunger pain was good.

All through high school, I was starving, then I would eat, and it was back and forth. You know: up, down, up, down. I would starve myself for a while and feel so deprived that I just— boom—would be off and running for food. I don't know what triggered it, but all of a sudden I'd feel deprived and think, "Well, I'm not accepted anyway, so why am I starving myself?" Then I would eat.

Graduating to Cocaine and Marriage

When I was in high school, I was hanging around with a girl, and we met a group of people who were a lot older than we were. I guess it must have been my junior year. I started dating a guy who dealt coke to all our friends, and, of course, I got into cocaine. I was dating him for three years, and it was a really sick relationship. I thrived on his insults. His telling me that I was no good, that I was fat, whatever. He had a problem also. But he used to say he didn't have a choice. Then he had to go into the reserves for the military, and he left. When he came back, we were seeing each other, and I had gained a lot of weight while he was gone, a lot. God, I don't even know why or what happened, but I had gone to the highest weight I had ever been. I was about 205 or something when he came back. He started working on a new job, and he met a girl at that job. He broke up with me. I had been out of high school for about eleven months. When he broke up with me he told me that if I lost 30 pounds he would marry me. And I proceeded to lose 30 pounds in a month and a half. By September I had an engagement ring on my finger, and by the following July I was married.

I lost the 30 pounds. I went on a liquid diet. I ended up in the hospital from it. I couldn't go to the bathroom from this, one of my crazy diets. And then I got out and we were engaged. We were planning the wedding, everything. I knew as I was walking down the aisle that the only reason I was marrying him was to hurt him more than he had hurt me, because the pain I felt when he told me he would marry me if I would lose 30 pounds, I can't even describe.

Starting Out Badly

I started drinking and using a lot more during the period I was on that diet and losing all that weight. By this time I was working full time. I had one job for eight months, and then the company was going under so I found another job. I started working there in October. The following July I got married, and it was like all hell broke loose. I walked down the aisle knowing that I wanted to hurt him more than he had hurt me. That backfired, of course. We went on our honeymoon, and things just started off bad. It was like, "There is no way this is ever going to work." We got married in July, and in September we went to Hawaii. We went through the military because he was still in the reserves. He was on base and I was in Waikiki by myself, and all of a sudden something in my head clicked: "Hey, you can take care of yourself. Here you are in Hawaii, and you're okay." It was the first time I had done anything by myself. It gave me an independent feeling I'd never felt before, that I liked. Then he lost his job, his regular job, in October. He was fired because of his mouth and because of his drinking.

The Insanity Really Starts

Throughout this, I was compulsively eating. I was drinking and I was eating. I was putting on weight, unbelievably. By November I was working two jobs, and as in everything else, I was a workaholic. I'd work eight hours at one job and then I would sell at night. I had a nervous breakdown. I was never put away for it, but the doctors prescribed a tranquilizer. When I got married, I kind of said to myself, "I'm going to stop drugging and stop drinking." Using the tranquilizers triggered me back into drugs. For two weeks, I took it a couple of times a day. Then I said, "This is crazy, I'm going to get hooked." And I threw them in the garbage. But two or three weeks later, I was back using cocaine full force, lying to my husband. My weight was going up, so, of course, I was trying to control my weight again, and the cocaine was going to do that. I would never tell my husband how much money I was making. I wouldn't tell him when I was taking money out. By February I was having an affair and was into drugs and alcohol. You couldn't stop me. I was like a fish with alcohol. I found someone who was selling coke on the job. I was getting it from him. I met a loan shark. This is where the insanity comes in.

In May I kicked my husband out of the house, so I was living alone in the apartment. By now I was not even eating. The only time I would eat is if someone brought food over for me. And if I did eat, it was only instant mashed potatoes. I was drinking and using cocaine all the way. I was still seeing the guy I was having the affair with, who I saw until I went into treatment. I was sick. I couldn't do anything. I would go out and get drunk and come home. I was just really scared, really alone.

After I kicked my husband out, I quit the nighttime job and just worked during the day. It was interfering with my drinking and my drugging, so, of course, I had to quit. Yes, that's really what it was, it was interfering with my time for drinking. But I wasn't eating now. Right after we got married, I was starting to have bowel problems. I was constipated all the time, and I learned this trick. When I went to the doctor, they would prescribe stool softeners. So I was using stool softeners to make me go to the bathroom and lose weight, and not eating. That's where the bulimia really clicked.

Moving Back with Mom and Dad

At the end of September, two years ago, my divorce was final. I lost my friendship with my mother. That Mother's Day I didn't even talk to her because my ex-husband would go to her and tell her my problems and come back to me and say, "Well, your mother said this," and "Your mother said that." So I totally cut off my family.

Then, somehow (my mom's a very spiritual person), my mom and dad asked me to move back home. I thought, "If I move back home, I won't have rent, so I can save all this money and be able to live by myself." Well, the whole time I was there, I couldn't save any money whatever. Any money I had went for drugs, food, cheap hotel rooms, that's it. When I moved back home, it was as if I just kept getting worse. The night I kicked my husband out, I looked at him and told him he was an alcoholic. He looked at me and said, "You're a coke addict." And I didn't like that, because it scared me. I told myself I was not an addict. I did not have a problem. I was in control.

Introduction to Heroin

After he left me in July, I started using heroin. I thought I wasn't worth anything. It was like, "Hey, why not? Why not? You know, you have nothing else to live for, and you're a piece of crap anyway." So I started with heroin. I was using heroin for a while, a year and four months, when I went into treatment. It went quick—I lost everything.

I got introduced to heroin through the guy I had the affair with. He used to deal it, but he was, I should say is, a heroin addict. It was his drug of choice. I remember the day I found that he did it, I went off the handle. I said, "I can't believe you would do that, blah, blah, blah, blah, blah." A month later, *I* was using.

I started out snorting it. I was snorting it the whole time. I wasn't shooting it. I was living with my mom and dad, I was hanging out on the south side of the city. I was in basements with cockroaches crawling all over. I didn't care. I just couldn't care anymore what I looked like. As long as I had money to eat and get high, I was okay. I would get up in the morning and figure out where I was going to get my money. I needed to have money to get high and also to eat. By then it was not one or the other, but both.

I continued to work through all this. Because I was living at home the only expenses I had were $230 a month. That was all that I ever had to be responsible for, but I was always broke. Everything else was going toward drugs and food.

I Was Always Broke

My parents didn't know what was going on. My dad made fun of me once about doing drugs. Of course I lied. I was the best con artist there was. "No, dad, I'm not doing drugs. I don't do drugs at all." But as my dad says, they were in denial too. They can admit that today. But back then, they could never figure out why I was always broke. I made about $20,000 a year and never had any money. They couldn't figure out why. My dad always used to say, jokingly, to my mom, "She must be doing drugs or something." While this was going on, if I didn't have enough money to get high and for food, I would steal food from their house. I would steal things. I was living with them, but I would steal food. I would take it out of the house so they wouldn't know.

Hiding and Eating

There were a couple of incidents with food that are really significant before I hit bottom. One, I went with my girfriend to her friend's house in the country, and I brought a box of candy for these people for letting us stay at their house. This is unbelievable, I owe these people great amends, but I found myself, while everyone was outside and I was inside, eating almost the whole box of candy. I think I left three pieces in there. I also ate two or three sandwiches while everyone was outside. I watched out the window, making sure no one was going to catch me. That whole trip was food. I ate from the time I left the city to the time I got there, and the whole time I was there. That hiding, and that feeling like, oh God, they are going to catch me, and that dishonesty—it was horrible!

There was also an experience with my mother, who had bought one of those chocolate candy bars, you know, the big ones. She bought one for my sister and one for my brother, but the one for my brother she never gave to him. By this time when I was home I would be up in my bedroom, nowhere else. I would not be with anyone else. She brought the candy bar up to split with me. And my little sister came home, and said, "What are you guys doing up there?" And I hid the candy bar and told her "nothing." My mom is laughing, and I'm hiding the candy bar. My sister went downstairs, then snuck back up and saw us eating the candy bar—she caught us. See, I wouldn't give it up. It was mine. I would isolate myself in my bedroom. It was a big room, I had the TV on. It was a soothing feeling, eating my food by myself.

People would say to me, "You need to lose weight." And the more they would tell me that, the more I would eat. Because it hurt. I knew I had to lose weight. I knew I was overweight, but I couldn't stop eating. And I didn't know why. I really didn't know why, until I went to treatment.

I Was Just Looking to Die

I wasn't drinking at that time. When I started using the heroin, I stopped drinking. That's why they had such a hard time convincing me I was an alcoholic, because for a year and four months I hadn't picked up a drink. I would drive down to the city, usually with food in my car. I would go right to the dope man, sit down there, get high, and usually get food to drive myself back up here, because it was another thirty-five-minute drive. It was sick. It was really bad. I was in places that I never even dreamt of. I never even knew places like this existed.

Having guys with guns in my car. Stupid stuff. You know, people would tell me not to go into a place, and I'd go in it. The more people told me not to go into these neighborhoods, that was where I went. It was like I was just looking to die. Waiting for someone to do it for me, because I was too chicken to do it myself.

The Weekend I Hit Bottom

My accident was the end of a weekend thing. It started on a Friday night. It was raining really hard. The guy I was seeing, who was living with another girl, told me he would try to see me Friday night. I was going to go down and see him. Then he called me, and I could tell he was drunk and high, and I got really angry. I had gotten paid, so I had money. I got in the car, and it was pouring, pouring rain. I drove down to the city, crying hysterically. I wanted to die. Going through my head were thoughts that he was living with another woman, and she had two of his kids. I was going to his house, and I was so mad that, if he had a gun, I was going to get it and blow him away. I also knew that he had a knife. I walked into his house a wreck, crying hysterically, and crazy, flipped out. The poor guy didn't know what to do. I was running through his house looking for the knife. I weighed about 210 when I went into treatment, so that's what I weighed that night, and he was a lot smaller than I was. He was struggling with me because I was going to get the knife and kill him. We fought a while, then I stopped and went right to the phone and called the dope dealer, who said he was leaving in ten minutes. I said "I'll come there, don't leave." But the dope dealer came to the house anyway. All of a sudden it was like, everything is okay again, because he brought drugs. I got high that whole weekend.

Then I went there to watch Monday night football. I was to meet two friends from work who had to work overtime. I couldn't wait. I picked up another friend, who was late. The game was going to start and I couldn't wait to get high. I tried, and I just couldn't wait for the others. So we went to the dope dealer's house and got the drugs, spending all the money I got paid on Friday. By this time I was totally broke. I hadn't paid any of my bills. Nothing.

Monday night I spent the last of my money, and that night something happened. I've never had this feeling before. I had always thought I was in control of my drugs, but that night I couldn't stop. I used everything I had, and then when the dealer showed up, he had some more, and I did it all. I didn't care about anyone else. I didn't care if it was their drugs, their money, their anything. I couldn't stop. I felt the control of the drugs over me. The next morning is when it happened—I was driving home and woke up almost underneath the semi. And I just asked for help. I remember screaming in my car, by myself, that I needed help.

Treatment—Learning How to Eat

In treatment, they put me on a food plan which involved no sugar, no flour. Three meals a day, a snack at night, nothing in between except coffee and diet pop. I went through a sugar withdrawal. They did all my meal plans for me up until my last day or two. Everything was done for me, which was good. I remember going to group the first day I was there. I was in with anorexics, who I hated my whole life and who were complaining about there being too much food to eat. I just could not comprehend something like that. But I had a hard time eating all the food they were giving me, too. I would have a salad, a vegetable, a starch, a protein (3 ounces of protein), a fruit and milk. It was food I wasn't used to eating.

They had me eating foods your body has to digest. I was used to eating junk. It was difficult for me. I asked for a lot of help. When I first went into treatment, for me to eat lunch or dinner took a half hour to forty-five minutes. It was good. I started eating foods that I thought I never liked, which I like today. I realize that this is how normal people eat. They had me look at myself. They had me look at my patterns, at "when do you eat." *I know I eat when I am feeling physical and mental pain.* I did a food history; talked about my particular binge foods. I could binge on anything, but starches, especially. I was a fantastic baker. When I baked, I would bake three things. One would be in the bedroom with me, and I would get mad if anyone ate the other two.

My Weight Will Be What God Wants It To Be

It really made me look at me and the pain I felt from not feeling a part of things. The most important thing I realized was that as long as I am abstinent today, my weight is going to be whatever God wants it to be. I learned not to make myself live by the scale, and not make my feelings depend upon what I think I look like.

I have a distorted self-image. When I'm really heavy, I don't believe I'm that heavy. When I'm thinner, I see myself as heavier. This still happens to me. Just last week, I put on an outfit and looked in the mirror and thought, "Wow, this looks great!" I turned away and looked back, and there was this huge person in the mirror. The distorted self-image is still there. But I'm aware of it today. That's the difference. I'm aware that now, when I'm going through a hard time emotionally, what I have to do is not eat. I ask for help today. I have a really close friend who I call up, and I tell her, "I'm in this place right now. I'm hurting, and I'm not going to eat. I need your help—will you come eat with me?" I can do that today.

A Sick Person Trying to Get Well

Treatment got me to look at myself through my eating history—when I ate, why I ate, what I ate. A lot of it came in aftercare treatment. A lot of my awareness today came through going to residential aftercare.

There, we had both group and individual treatment. I saw my

counselor once every two weeks. But there was group every night, and then there was a small group once a week. Everyone I was in group with had eating disorders and was dealing with this. It's really hard to go from the controlled environment in treatment to having to do it yourself, without controlling your food plan. It's like your body goes into shock. You think, "Oh, my God, I don't know what to do. I don't know what to eat."

One thing I found out is, "keep it simple." I know what is right for me to eat. I know what is not. I know what no one else does: I know what is going to trigger me off. I know what portions are comfortable for me today. I think the most important thing is I'm eating to live, not living to eat. I found that through treatment. Also, through treatment I realized I was thinking that I'm a bad person trying to get good. I came to the understanding that I'm a sick person trying to get well. That's really important for me, because once I get back into that "good and bad" stuff, my thinking is gone.

When I went to aftercare, I was told it was a place for me to build the foundation of my program, and that's what I set out to do. I feel I accomplished that. I went to my groups. I was with people who had been in aftercare, but I was looking to the outside, too. I needed my outside support system because I knew I was going to be out there soon, so I started going to outside meetings. I got two sponsors.

I go to one OA meeting a week. When I was in aftercare, I went to one or two. I find, right now, I need to go to one OA, two CA (Cocaine Anonymous), and two AA meetings a week. If I'm having a hard time with food, I go to an OA meeting. But today I can go to an AA meeting, and, if I am having trouble with my food, hear in an AA meeting what I need to hear about food. I don't have a hard time with that. I know a lot of people do, but I don't, because it's all the same to me. Both of my sponsors are AA and OA, which is really good for me. I need people who are aware of my eating and my life. Because that for me is the first thing to go. If I am having a hard time, my head tells me, "Well, it's okay to eat this," when it is not okay. I am trying to stuff my feelings, but my head tells me that food is not as bad as drugs. I'll begin to believe it's okay to pick up food instead of picking up a drug, and it's not okay—because once I do that, it will lead me right back to drugs.

Family Participation

My family participated in treatment, too. We would have one or two counseling sessions with my mom and dad, and one with my brother and sister. It was kind of neat, because my mom and dad took it upon themselves to be a part of it. For the first time in my life I felt like my dad was a part of my life. Everything he could come to—he'd be there. And I knew he loved me. It was really neat. We talked. We talked in family discussion about my feelings, about my always feeling he wanted me to be a boy. And he voiced his feelings, and it was just really, really healthy. Everyone got their feelings out. They have a family retreat program through there, and my mom went on that. My dad was not able to, but my mom went. They started going to open meetings with me while I was in treatment, and they were at the meeting with me today. They go with me to my open meetings once a month. We were able to talk honestly about what happened and where I was, and sometimes I can feel the pain in my mom. I was really glad she didn't know what was wrong with me. She had no idea about what was going on in my life, and she did a lot of praying for me. I am really grateful for that. Because God would stand in there for me. I think she was relieved to know that I was sick and that I could get better—you know, that I had a disease—a real relief inside of her.

Eating Illness Is as Severe as Alcohol or Drug Addiction

I remember something that was engraved in my head at aftercare by my counselor. He said, "If you don't deal with this eating disorder, you will end up using again, dead, or in a mental institution. I know, and I've seen it." This is why residential aftercare was so good for me. One of my roommates couldn't deal with her bulimia, and started drinking while she was there. I saw that and I lived through it. My other roommate could not deal with her eating disorder and ended up on a mental ward. People laugh about it sometimes, and I get really angry, because I've seen it. I know what will happen to me if I don't deal with it. Last week a person really close to me called and asked about eating disorders because his friend is schizoed out. She can't talk or say more than two words. That's how powerful this eating stuff is. People don't realize it. This can kill you. I guess the most important thing that I learned through treatment is that this disease is going to kill me if I don't take care of myself. It's just as severe as alcohol or drug addiction, and it's probably my primary disease. I believe today that without taking care of the eating disorder, I would definitely be out there using. I'd be out there dead.

Giving Up the Old Crowd

When I went into treatment, I gave up my old crowd. When I was in treatment the guy I'd been going with kept trying to see me, and when I was in treatment they forbade me to see him. I called him up and told him if I kept seeing him I was going to relapse. I'd had it. I knew I was going to die. It was really hard, but I had to. I didn't see him because they told me not to, but I was really afraid I'd give in. Later, there were a couple of times when I did see him. I had to find out for myself that it was sick.

The thing that triggered me that it was a sick relationship was when he said to me, "You don't have to change. I'll marry you just the way you are." And I thought, "Oh, my God!" I *want* to change today. That's where the difference is. I don't want to be like that anymore. And that was the beginning of total surrender to my problem. Not thinking, "Well, some day." Because I went for six months thinking, "Maybe if he could just get the program things would work out." I actually took him to treatment. He stayed only three days. He's not ready yet.

For me it was a process of being able to surrender totally. Now other people, like the girl I was telling you about who I'd been friends with since I was three years old, are back in my life.

New Relationships—The Ache Inside is Gone

I think the neatest thing is that my old friend is back in my life today, after all these years of not even wanting to be acquainted. And I have new friends. Everyone I associate with now, except for the people at work, are program people, and I need that today because we have something in common.

That ache inside of me is gone. You know, that lonely ache of always feeling you're alone and never feeling a part of things, is gone. For the first time in my life I feel like people will understand me and love me no matter what I do. Right or wrong, they're going to accept me and love me, and they let me be me. That's really neat.

Until now, I've never met people who can tell me, "Yeah, I've been through that before, I know this is what I do to get out of it"—except for people in the program. "Feel the feelings, it's okay." You know, it *is* okay to feel the feelings—just don't act on them today. I remember that when things are bad, and I remember I'm not a bad person because I'm feeling this way. Before, if I was angry or hurt, I was never able to tell anyone I was hurt. Today I'm getting better. I might not be able to do it right away, but today I am able to say, "Hey, I'm really hurt by this."

My life has changed totally in the last eleven months, and God has put people in my life who are in Twelve Step programs, such as CA or AA, who have an active eating disorder but are not aware of it because they went to a treatment center that doesn't deal with eating disorders. I talk to them and work with them, and it's tough. It's really tough. I hate to say that it's harder than dealing with alcoholism, but, man, it's so difficult. Food is an everyday part of my life, and an everyday part of other people's lives. I find that dishonesty and poor self-esteem in people with eating disorders is a lot worse than in someone who is only alcoholic.

I heard on the radio that about eighty percent of the population has an eating disorder. I thought that was pretty much right on target, because I don't think people understand. Like I told my boss, eating disorders today are like alcoholism was thirty and forty years ago—people just don't understand.

Part of it comes with how we are raised. You eat too much or eat everything on your plate. Being told to lose weight your whole life, looking at magazines, seeing people on TV—oh, this beautiful woman on this commerical—and she is probably anorexic. That's how people are gearing their thoughts.

What I find with men is that they are just coming out of the closet on eating disorders. Like when alcoholism first began being publicized, it was primarily men, and then all of a sudden women started coming out. I was in treatment with a man who was bulimic, who binged and purged. My uncle went through treatment for alcoholism. Now, he goes to the Twelve Step program, but I find that he has turned his addiction right into food. All he eats is sugar. He is blowing up, and I think the tendency is high for a man to turn to food after alcohol is taken away from him. Women, too.

When I was in treatment, a counselor said, "I think that one day alcoholism and eating disorders will be dealt with as one." I believe that. It seems true for a lot of people I see. One of my sponsors had been in AA for eight years, and she was in chronic depression and wanting to kill herself—because of an eating disorder that was not being dealt with. It took her a lot of work to turn around. She could not figure it out. Here she was, working this program and working the Twelve Steps, and it was not helping because she wasn't working on the eating disorder.

The Program Supports Me

The support I get from my program is fantastic. When I first went into aftercare, I was there for two months, and I was having stomach attacks. They thought I was having appendicitis. I ended up at a hospital. I told them I was bulimic, a compulsive overeater, a drug addict, and alcoholic—and they gave me nothing by mouth for two days. At the end of two days, I was not having appendicitis, but I was still having pains. When they put food in front of me, I went anorexic. After two days of nothing by mouth, they put food in front of me and I would not eat. It wasn't that I couldn't, you see. The doctors and nurses, because they didn't know, thought I couldn't eat, so there must be something wrong with me. It's not that I couldn't—I wouldn't. My thinking was all the way gone.

When my sponsors walked in, I was hysterical. They said, "What do you want? What sounds good to you right now?" I said Chinese food. They went and they go me Chinese food and made me eat it while they were sitting there. And they told the staff, "This girl's thinking is gone. She is actively, totally back to the anorexic side. She needs to be with us." They took me out of the hospital at eight o'clock at night, called the doctors, and said, "She's got to get out of here. She needs to be in a meeting. She needs to be with people who understand what is going on inside of her." I went and spent the next two nights at my sponsor's house. They wouldn't leave me alone. This is the love that I found here.

I Feel Accepted.

I think the most important thing for me, as I said before, is that the awful ache is gone. I have the Twelve Step Program, and I am accepted. I feel accepted. I feel a part of things. I am capable of being honest today, of sharing "me" with other people, and it's only through the Twelve Steps and the groups that I belong to, the programs that I belong to. I think that's really important. I need to remember that I have to deal with all three of my addictions in the three different programs. I need to go to AA and talk about my experiences in drinking and those feelings and to hear other people; go to OA and talk about food and hear about food; go to CA and talk about drugs. You know, they are all similar, and they all do the same thing, but there are different little tricks that we all play in the different categories. I need to remember that. That's why I need to go to all three. That's why I need the balance in my program.

Working on Recovery

I would not give up what I have today for anything. Because it is unbelievable. I have God in my life. And I trust Him, I have faith that no matter what happens today, He'll be there for me. I remember that, and nothing can be so bad that I need to get over it with food or chemicals. Then He and I together can begin to handle it.

I have tools. I have my writing. I have my roommate. My sponsor. I find there is something else that a counselor told me, and I'll always remember this. "When a compulsive overeater is feeling hungry and it's not time to be feeling hungry yet, probably the only thing they need is a hug." Today I am able to ask for that. When I'm feeling that, I'm able to ask for that. And say, "Hey, I need a hug!" That's really neat.

I have to live this program one day at a time. Once I heard a sponsor asking my friend, "What have you done today for your recovery?" I have to remember that every day. Just today—it's just today. All I have is just today. What have I done today for my recovery? Then I write in my books: "Have I stayed abstinent? Have I gone to my meetings? Have I written? Have I called my sponsor? What have I done today for my recovery?" Because whatever I do today for my recovery is something good for me.

Even though I've only been around eleven months, I've been through a lot. When I came in the program, I had four grandparents living and one great-grandmother living. Today I only have two grandparents. All since I've been sober. I feel God got me sober before this happened, so that I could live through it instead of "exist" through it.

I believe that today I need to be involved. Although sometimes I have a hard time saying no, I'm trying to learn how. Yesterday I said it. They asked me to be secretary of the meeting, and I realized that I would cheat by doing too much right now. I need time to think, time for me—because it is really easy for me to get into something else and not take a look at me. The focus needs to be on me, not all the time, but I need to be aware of what is going on with me, and not just doing all these "things" all the time. My mom and dad always had something to do and they were always busy, busy, busy. I could never understand that. I'd sit up in my room, and I could never understand why and how they were always so busy. Today I do. It was a method of denial.

Learning to Trust

There is something else that is really important to me in this program: when I'm hurting, I have friends today who know I'm hurting and call at home, just to see if I'm okay. They'll call me up and ask, "Did you get through last night okay?" That's something that I never had or felt before, and every time it happens, I get this warm feeling, and I realize this is how it works. We care and we love each other, unconditionally. No matter what we are going through, we're very best friends.

I had to work toward trusting people very slowly. I know today when certain people walk into my life, I can't just trust them right off. It's kind of a process where little things will happen, and then my trust will get stronger. I had an experience when I was in residential aftercare. A girl told me that she had switched the phone over to her name when I was moving out, and I found out a couple of weeks later that she didn't. I trusted her, and I was really upset.

But it helped me to talk to a lady who has eleven years in the program. She said that even though this is a trusting program, sometimes people have to prove their trust to us. Little things need to happen for us to trust. Because we were all liars, cheats, cons, you know, so we need to rebuild that trust. That was a real learning experience, very much so.

When I first went into treatment, I trusted everything they told me. I was willing to do whatever they told me. I trusted whatever they said. I believed it and I did it. It's a joke with my friends, you know. Sometimes I wonder, "Yeah, why did I do this?" Today I really and truly believe that God gave me that willingness, because if I didn't have it, I would die. And He wants me to be alive. I want to be alive.

Conclusion

After reading the seven stories in the book, you have seen the whole spectrum of eating disorders—from Jody with a snacking problem to Pat with multiple addictions. You have seen the work of recovery, bringing not only abstinence but also many new personal and spiritual dimensions to the lives of recovering people. You now have enough information to decide for yourself:

- Do you have a "weight problem" or do you have a behavior problem?
- Has dieting changed your eating behavior, or has it temporarily diminished the symptoms?
- Are you ready for a real solution to the real problem?

As the seven people in this book have demonstrated, there is a solution. It isn't a "quick fix." It is a personal challenge requiring honesty, courage, and self-acceptance. Most of all, it requires the desire to do it. When you want it badly enough, a new life will be there for you.